MW00785827

You're Hired!

SPECIAL EDUCATION LAW, POLICY, AND PRACTICE

Series Editors

Mitchell L. Yell, PhD, University of South Carolina
David F. Bateman, PhD, Shippensburg University of Pennsylvania

The Special Education Law, Policy, and Practice series highlights current trends and legal issues in the education of students with disabilities. The books in this series link legal requirements with evidence-based instruction and highlight practical applications for working with students with disabilities. The titles in the Special Education Law, Policy, and Practice series are designed not only to be required textbooks for general education and special education preservice teacher education programs but are also designed for practicing teachers, education administrators, principals, school counselors, school psychologists, parents, and others interested in improving the lives of students with disabilities. The Special Education Law, Policy, and Practice series is committed to research-based practices working to provide appropriate and meaningful educational programming for students with disabilities and their families.

Titles in Series

You're Hired!

Practical Strategies for
Guiding Individuals with
Autism Spectrum Disorder to
Competitive Employment

Patricia S. Arter
Winthrop University

Tammy B. H. Brown
Marywood University

Jennifer Barna
Marywood University

ROWMAN & LITTLEFIELD
Lanham • Boulder • New York • London

Executive Acquisitions Editor: Mark Kerr
Assistant Acquisitions Editor: Sarah Rinehart
Sales and Marketing Inquiries: textbooks@rowman.com

Published by Rowman & Littlefield
An imprint of The Rowman & Littlefield Publishing Group, Inc.
4501 Forbes Boulevard, Suite 200, Lanham, Maryland 20706
www.rowman.com

86-90 Paul Street, London EC2A 4NE

Copyright © 2024 by The Rowman & Littlefield Publishing Group, Inc.

All rights reserved. No part of this book may be reproduced in any form or by any
electronic or mechanical means, including information storage and retrieval systems,
without written permission from the publisher, except by a reviewer who may quote
passages in a review.

British Library Cataloguing in Publication Information Available

Library of Congress Cataloging-in-Publication Data Available
ISBN 978-1-5381-7740-2 (cloth)
ISBN 978-1-5381-7741-9 (paper)
ISBN 978-1-5381-7742-6 (ebook)

♾️™ The paper used in this publication meets the minimum requirements of American
National Standard for Information Sciences—Permanence of Paper for Printed Library
Materials, ANSI/NISO Z39.48-1992.

Contents

CHAPTER 1

Autism Spectrum Disorder and Employment

···

Petra is an 18-year-old female with ASD who attends her area high school. Petra has strong verbal skills and is able to accurately read facial expressions and body language of the speaker. Petra has never had paid employment and her vocational training is limited. Petra wants to be a teaching assistant at her high school when she graduates next year.

THINGS TO THINK ABOUT

- What type of preparation has Petra had to help her meet her goals?
- Are employers open to hiring autistic individuals? Why or why not?

Based on current statistics Petra most likely has less than a 50% chance of finding any type of employment, let alone competitive employment that fits her interests, strengths, and preferences. Without gainful employment, Petra's quality-of-life outcomes greatly decline.

Watch this TED talk where Claire Barnett from Vanderbilt talks about why autistic unemployment is so high: https://youtu.be/FVZu557_k04.

EMPLOYMENT STATISTICS

According to the Individuals with Disabilities Education Improvement Act (IDEA, 2004), public education should prepare an individual for employment. Individuals with disabilities should have the same access to the rights and entitlements of the rest of society, including employment. Employment enables individuals to earn a living wage to support themselves and pursue their interests. Additionally, employment helps provide the individual with a sense of personal dignity and self-efficacy that improves confidence, contributes to overall well-being, and leads to better quality-of-life outcomes. Moreover, increased employment rates for individuals with and without disabilities reduce the societal costs by reducing reliance on government support and increasing productivity.

···

Unfortunately, it is often challenging for individuals with disabilities to find and sustain employment. Approximately 35% of individuals with disabilities are employed, compared to 76% of individuals without disabilities (Bonaccio et al., 2020). Those who are employed are often underemployed, sometimes only part-time, and earn a lower-than-average salary. In 2021, only 19.1% of persons with a disability were employed. Although this is up from 17.9% in 2020 (Bureau of Labor Statistics, 2022), individuals with disabilities are not afforded the same access to employment as their nondisabled peers. Although it is evident that unemployment is a challenge faced by most individuals with disabilities, young adults with autism spectrum disorder (ASD) appear to be at a higher risk for unemployment when compared to other disability categories. In fact, young adults with ASD were least likely (45.2%) of all 12 disability categories to be paid for work outside the home and though they comprised the largest transition-aged group to seek vocational rehabilitation services, they had the worst outcomes (Sanford et al., 2011).

Autism first became its own diagnosis in the *Diagnostic Statistical Manual of Mental Disorders* (*DSM-III*) in 1980. In 1991, the U.S. Department of Education ruled that a diagnosis of autism qualifies a student for special education services. Before this additional disability category was added, many students with autism were classified as intellectually disabled. Since that time, with increased awareness and diagnosis, rates of ASD have rapidly increased. In 2021, the Centers for Disease Control and Prevention (CDC) reported that approximately one in 44 U.S. children were diagnosed with ASD (CDC, 2022). It should also be noted that symptoms may have been masked for some students with high-functioning autism (HFA). These students may never have been diagnosed or received services. Additionally, some students with HFA may have been diagnosed with Asperger's syndrome under the *DSM-IV* criteria, but under *DSM-V* autism spectrum disorders level-1 services, they may not be provided the services for transition that they need. Overall, as schools increased awareness and identification, services and programs slowly began to develop. While currently there are a plethora of services for early intervention and school-aged children, program development has not yet met the demand of the rapidly increasing transition-age and adult ASD population.

There is an estimated 2.21% or 5,437,988 adults in the United States who have ASD (CDC, 2022). Fewer than half of adults with autism are employed. Those who are employed work only part-time or are overqualified for the job they are working. According to the 2017 *National Autism Indicators Report*, across a sample of adults with ASD who received developmental disability services, only 14% achieved work in an integrated setting, while 54% worked without pay in a segregated setting (Roux et al., 2017). The National Longitudinal Study-2 (NLTS-2) indicated that four out of 10 young adults with ASD never worked for pay in their young adulthood (Roux et al., 2017). It is imperative that educators work with individuals with ASD prior to leaving high school to help facilitate a successful transition to employment. The Individuals with Disabilities Education Improvement Act (IDEA, 2004) requires transition services: begin by age

16; be student-driven by the student's goals; be individualized based on the student's needs, strengths, interests, and preferences; and include opportunities for functional skills for work and community life. Transition to adult services such as job support programs and adult services specific to ASD are limited. Unlike IDEA, adult services are not entitlements; they are services for which an applicant must apply and be eligible. Most current job support programs are for intellectual or physical disabilities and are sheltered workshops, though supportive or competitive employment has the best outcomes. Schools need to work with students with ASD to access and apply for these services prior to leaving high school.

CHARACTERISTICS OF ASD: EMPLOYMENT CHALLENGES AND STRENGTHS

Challenges

The primary characteristics of ASD include: (1) poorly developed social skills; (2) difficulty with expressive and receptive language; and (3) the presence of restrictive and repetitive behaviors. Since ASD is a "spectrum," individual characteristics will vary greatly within each of these categories. While these characteristics need to be considered, schools and families must be careful not to have lower expectations. Lower expectations can lead to less opportunity to learn and practice necessary skills and can impact the confidence of the individual. In order for individuals with ASD to be prepared for competitive employment, their unique needs, strengths, interests, and preferences must be fully considered as we train them so they can successfully transition to employment. This can be quite challenging, given that many of these characteristics impact the ability to interview effectively and then to secure and maintain employment.

Specific challenges in securing and maintaining employment might include unusual eye contact, stereotypic movements, lack of reciprocity in conversation, and misunderstood figurative language leading to responses that employers and coworkers might feel are inappropriate or undesirable. Social impairments can include inappropriate hygiene or grooming skills, inappropriate comments to members of the opposite sex, inability to understand affect, and difficulty working alone (Hendricks, 2010). Inflexibility makes it difficult to handle changing schedules or new job responsibilities. Physical environment and sensory challenges, such as sensitivity to light, sound, or stimuli might make the work environment challenging or increase stress and anxiety for the individual with ASD. Compromised social or expressive language skills might prevent an individual with ASD from properly articulating their strengths or needs or understanding everyday social interactions with customers, a supervisor, or coworkers. High levels of social anxiety can prove to be a barrier that impacts job performance if the individual doesn't clearly understand the task, or if they are untrained or unprepared to complete a required task, which in turn may lead to challenging behaviors. Table 1.1 illustrates how ASD might manifest as challenging in the workplace.

TABLE 1.1. Challenges Presented by ASD in Workplace

Characteristics of Autism Spectrum	*How It Might Manifest as a Challenge*
Poorly developed social skills	• Inappropriate hygiene or grooming skills: not combing hair or showering; not wearing a uniform as required • Inappropriate comments to members of the opposite sex: misinterpreting friendship and asking for a date • Inappropriate responses to coworkers—may be seen as blunt or rude
Difficulty with expressive and receptive language	• Inability to articulate needs • Lack of reciprocity in conversation: conversation is one-sided; answers questions as "yes" or "no" • Unusual eye contact: no eye contact or staring • Misunderstood figurative language: "I could eat a horse"; "I need that like a hole in the head"
Restrictive and repetitive behaviors	• Stereotypic movements: pacing, rocking • Unwillingness to talk about anything other than his/her specific interests • Inflexibility: unwillingness to change schedule or job tasks
Sensory challenges	• Noise: beeping of a forklift as it backs up in the warehouse; a dissatisfied customer raising voice • Competing stimuli: multiple phones ringing, customers asking questions, intercom announcements • Refusal to wear appropriate clothing or safety gear due to sensitivity

Strengths

The potential for individuals with ASD in the workplace is largely unrealized given the unemployment and underemployment statistics. While there may be challenges to hiring an individual with ASD, building on the individual's strengths can provide the employer with a valuable employee. Individuals with ASD often possess skills and abilities that are highly valued in many industries. Employers value reliability, trustworthiness, low absenteeism, and punctuality. Strengths of individuals with ASD often include attention to detail and intense focus. Once they learn a job task, they are reliable and consistent in their performance. They often prefer performing tasks of a repetitive nature that other employees do not enjoy. Textbox 1.1 lists other possible desirable strengths of individuals with ASD in the workplace.

```
┌─────────────────────────────────────────────────────────────────────┐
│  TEXTBOX 1.1.   DESIRABLE STRENGTHS OF EMPLOYEES WITH ASD            │
│                                                                       │
│   • Attention to detail                                               │
│   • Goal-directed behavior                                            │
│   • Task focus                                                        │
│   • Passion                                                           │
│   • Loyalty                                                           │
│   • Reliability                                                       │
│   • Trustworthy and dependability                                     │
│   • Honesty                                                           │
│   • Ability to tolerate monotonous tasks                             │
│   • Low absenteeism                                                   │
│   • Good memory                                                       │
│   • Ability to adhere to routine                                      │
│   • Expertise in a certain area                                       │
│   • Technical abilities (e.g., computer skills)                       │
└─────────────────────────────────────────────────────────────────────┘
```

PROMISING PRACTICES AND FACTORS THAT LEAD TO SUCCESSFUL EMPLOYMENT

Inclusive Comprehensive Transition and Postsecondary Programs

The Higher Education Opportunity Act of 2008 (HEOA) created a new type of college program for students with intellectual disabilities called the Comprehensive Transition and Postsecondary (CTP) program. The HEOA, in Section § 668.231, defines a student with an intellectual disability as a student:

B. (1) with a cognitive impairment, characterized by significant limitations in—
   (i) intellectual and cognitive functioning; and
   (ii) adaptive behavior as expressed in conceptual, social, and practical adaptive skills; and
(2) who is currently, or was formerly, eligible for a free appropriate public education under the Individuals with Disabilities Education Act [20 U.S.C. 1400 et seq.].

The comprehensive transition and postsecondary programs target the provision of access to postsecondary education for those students with intellectual disabilities who traditionally have been unable to participate in higher education. If a student with autism spectrum disorder (ASD) also has a co-occurring documented intellectual disability (significant cognitive impairment with significant limitation in cognitive functioning, and limitations in adaptive behavior, and who was formerly or currently eligible for IDEA services), that student *does* meet the definition of an eligible student. The HEOA provides access to federal student aid for students attending approved CTP who have an intellectual disability even if they do not have a standard high school diploma and are not matriculating toward a degree.

Think College has a national network of CTP programs (https://thinkcollege.net/). There are more than 300 Think College programs nationwide. These inclusive higher-education programs are dedicated to developing, expanding, and improving research and practice in inclusive higher education for individuals with intellectual disabilities. Attending institutes of higher education allows students to strengthen their interpersonal skills, develop new friendships, and increase their independence. Think College programs support students and integrate academics, functional skills, self-determination, career development, and social experiences. Students enrolled in Think College programs are generally 18–26 years old; have an intellectual disability (as defined by HEOA); graduated from high school with a standard or alternate diploma; and exhibit sufficient communicative, social, and functional skills to navigate campus and the community with little to no support. Through Think College programs, students are able to access academic coursework, residential life, work, and social experiences that may not have been previously accessible to them. Inclusive higher education has been found to have a positive impact on the outcomes of graduates, including employment, residential life, and community participation. In fact, students with intellectual disabilities who participated in these inclusive programs were more likely to be employed and have higher earnings than their counterparts who did not participate in these experiences.

Autism Awareness

Hendricks (2010) indicates that the following factors contribute to success for individuals with ASD in the workplace:

1. The jobs need to be matched to the interests of the individual with ASD.
2. Employers need to provide adequate learning time with clearly defined tasks.
3. The environment needs to be predictable with minimal distractions and free from excess sensory stimuli.

In order for individuals with ASD to be successful on the job, it could be beneficial to self-disclose their diagnosis. Knowledge and understanding of ASD by coworkers is key in fostering successful workplace relationships (Dreaver et al., 2020). In order for individuals with ASD to be successfully employed, employers need to provide autism awareness training to supervisors and coworkers so there is an understanding of the characteristics of the employee with ASD (Dreaver et al., 2020). For example, providing education and awareness training regarding communication strategies, behaviors associated with ASD, and strategies to maximize strengths while minimizing the impact of challenging behaviors creates a more inclusive work environment (Dreaver et al., 2020). By understanding the characteristics, employers and coworkers may better match the employee with tasks that utilize their strengths. Additionally, awareness training helps avoid misinterpretation of behaviors. Employers who were educated in ASD learned to consider environmental conditions and provide ongoing support; continuous feedback; and succinct, clear, and explicit communication. Table 1.2 illustrates strategies and supports that facilitate successful employment for individuals with ASD (Dreaver et al., 2020).

TABLE 1.2. Strategies and Supports That Facilitate Successful Employment

Social	Adaptive Strategies	Cognitive Supports	Vocational Training Supports
• Additional supervision • Mentor support • Clear expectations • Explicit, clear Communication	• Written, step-by-step procedures • Routine and structure • Defined supervisor • Accommodations to sensory demands (dimming lights, noise reducing headphones)	• Reinforce positive behavior • Consistent feedback • Strategies to manage stress and anxiety	• Hygiene and personal care training • Job matching support • Realistic goal setting • Résumé/portfolio development • Interview skills training • Job application assistance

Transition Support Services and Training

> Tip: In Chapters 2 through 7, activities are provided to support the individual with ASD as they prepare for employment. Encourage the job seeker to create a Job Notebook with completed activities and resources.

Although training for employers, coworkers, and supervisors is needed, there is much the individual with ASD can do to promote a successful job search and initial employment experience. The chapters that follow will continue to expand upon these successful strategies. Successful employment depends on a variety of factors that will be discussed in this book. Each chapter will go more in depth on each topic and provide activities and resources for training. Individuals with ASD must be supported and explicitly trained in:

1. Identifying their strengths, abilities, and preferences, as well as their limitations and challenges (Chapter 2).
2. Setting realistic goals for employment (Chapter 2).
3. Choosing jobs that are matched to their interests, strengths, and abilities, and analyzing job tasks (Chapter 2).
4. Building a résumé and portfolio (Chapter 3).
5. Preparing and practicing for the job interview (Chapter 4).
6. Acting appropriately in the workplace with coworkers, supervisors, and customers (Chapter 5).
7. Handling conflict and challenges in the workplace (Chapter 6).
8. Understanding rights and responsibilities in the workplace (Chapter 7)
9. Self-advocacy (Chapter 7).

Preparing the Job Seeker

....

Teacher: What's your dream job?
Student: I'm going to be a rock star.

THINGS TO THINK ABOUT

- "You can be anything you put your mind to" is an oft-repeated mantra of encouragement as children and adolescents explore career possibilities. Is this encouragement appropriate for the job seeker with ASD? Why or why not?
- How would you respond to the job seeker with ASD who has his/her heart set on a career dream you feel is out of reach?
- What kinds of support benefit the individual with ASD as they look ahead to employment?

OVERVIEW OF THE JOB SEARCH PROCESS

Ask any kid what they want to be when they grow up, and they are sure to have an answer. Most dream jobs, like being a YouTube star or a professional musician, eventually evolve into more attainable roles, such as IT workers, medical personnel, or sales professionals. For the job seeker with ASD, grandiose plans may persist, but eventually it's time to put feet to the dream.

Though individuals with ASD have much to offer employers, repetitive or intense interests can complicate the selection of an appropriate job. Teachers and other caring adults may find strong resistance as they try to steer the individual with ASD toward a job that matches their interests but also presents a reasonable opportunity for the job seeker to be successful. In addition, communication challenges and executive functioning impairments affect multiple phases of the overall job search process. Given these challenges, the individual with ASD will likely need considerable support. Table 2.1 shows examples of how the job search process can be impacted by ASD.

The phases in the process of preparing the job seeker with ASD for employment are similar to those of any job seeker, though the level and kind of support needed at each phase of the process may differ. In addition, the steps may be recursive at times, rather than completely linear. For example, as the individual engages in the Career

....

TABLE 2.1. Potential Impact of ASD on the Job Search Process

Phase of Career Development	What Happens	When the Stage Predominantly Occurs	Potential Impact of ASD	Examples
Career Awareness	Developing awareness of the kinds of work people do	Preschool through high school	Children learn much about the work people do by engaging in social activities. The individual with ASD may have less exposure to the kinds of opportunities available.	The neurotypical child may participate in sports, clubs, and other social contexts where they encounter adults in a variety of jobs, whereas the child with ASD who has social anxiety may have had fewer encounters.
Personal Assessment: Identifying Strengths, Interests, and Challenges Related to Employment	Self-assessment and goal setting as a result of self-reflection, input from others, job-related research, and the use of various assessment tools	Middle school and high school	Difficulty with self-reflection; grandiose plans may persist, though unrealistic; perseverance makes it difficult to see alternatives; difficulty seeing the big picture; intense and restricted interests make it difficult to look at realistic options.	*Teacher:* What skills do you have? *Student:* I'm good at video games. I'm going to be a famous gamer.
Career Exploration	Refine goals by identifying potential matches between the individual and various jobs by comparing the demands of the jobs with the individual's personal profile	Elementary school through high school	Challenges in seeing the big picture, planning steps in a process, and prioritizing make it difficult to map out a workable career pathway.	*Student:* I'm going to be a veterinary assistant. *Teacher:* What do you need to do in order to become a veterinary assistant? *Student:* Well, I love animals.

| Career Preparation | Development of job search skills and skills needed on the job, including personal development, development of soft skills, vocational training, and/or education | High School and Post-High School | Communication challenges, including taking things literally, eye contact, failure to read facial cues, limitations in problem-solving abilities | *Problem:* The student has regular medical appointments every other Thursday afternoon but has been scheduled to work on a Thursday she is usually off. *Response:* Gets upset and anxious because of the conflict. |
| Career Pursuit | Networking, submission of résumés, and interviewing with the goal of successful employment | High School and Post-High School | Communication challenges can impact interview skills, as well as initial job experiences with supervisors and coworkers | *Interviewer:* Have you been waiting long? *Student:* Yes, I've been here for 17 minutes. |

Note. Phases of Career Development adapted from Morningstar & Clavenna-Deane (2018) and Bernick & Holden (2015).

Exploration phase, he or she may find the need to engage in further personal assessment to determine if a job is really a good fit. Or, if a job seeker in the Career Pursuit phase fails to secure a job in a timely manner, revisiting the Career Exploration and/or the Career Preparation phases may be appropriate. Furthermore, at each phase of the process, individuals with ASD need explicit instruction, as well as opportunities for guided application, as they tend not to pick up naturally on cues within their environment.

As explained in Chapter 1, individuals with ASD are more likely to be unemployed or underemployed than those in other disability groups. What are the predictors of success in postsecondary employment? According to the National Secondary Transition Technical Assistance Center, work-related experiences, including paid employment, vocational education, and work study, as well as inclusion in general education, ranked highest as predictors of success. Other factors that potentially predict success include career awareness opportunities, community-based experiences, occupational courses, parental involvement, self-advocacy/self-determination, self-care/independent living skills, and social skills development. Most current job support programs are for intellectual or physical disabilities and are sheltered workshops. However, supportive or competitive employment has the best outcomes. This chapter focuses on some practical ways to promote success by helping students to increase their career awareness and engage in personal assessment experiences that promote an improved ability to self-advocate and a sense of self-determination.

Activity 2.1: My Job Pathway

Begin assembling a job notebook to document progress in the job search process. Using Activity 2.1: My Job Pathway, review the phases of career development with students. Include My Job Pathway as the first page in the notebook. Students can circle or make notes on the phases as they work through them. Remind students that they can always revisit previous phases, as needed. Add activities and resources to the notebook to document progress toward employment goals.

CAREER AWARENESS

Developing an awareness of various careers begins in preschool and continues throughout life, but by high school, students usually have a sense of many types of jobs that exist. In addition, they often know the type of work they *do not* want to do. However, they may not have a clear idea of the kind of job they *want* to pursue. Because some individuals with ASD have not had the wide variety of social experiences or interests that their neurotypical peers may have had, and because they may not pick up on the information such experiences provide, the job seeker with ASD often benefits from career awareness activities, such as

- guest speakers from various professions,
- videos of individuals at work,
- field trips,
- job fairs, and
- career assessment. (Morningstar et al., 2012)

Experiences such as those listed are helpful, but not sufficient in and of themselves. The job seeker with ASD benefits from explicit guidance so they can profit from the experiences. For example, a teacher might prepare students for a guest speaker, video, job fair, field trip, or career assessment by giving them a checklist of things to listen or look for or questions to ask.

In addition, job seekers with ASD should become aware of companies that actively seek to hire individuals with disabilities, and consider applying to these companies. Walgreens, CVS, Home Depot, and Microsoft are just a few examples of employers that recognize the advantages of hiring individuals with ASD, while also taking steps to support those individuals (Solomon, 2020).

ACTIVITY 2.1. My Job Pathway

Name_____

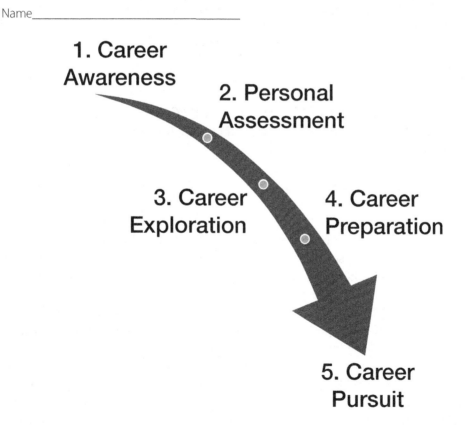

Note. Adapted from "Your complete guide to transition planning and services," by M. E. Morningstar & B. Clavenna-Deane (2018)

Activity 2.2: Job Fair Guidesheet

Use Activity 2.2: Job Fair Guidesheet to help the job seeker with ASD more strategically question potential employers about job qualifications and determine whether they are a good fit for the position.

ACTIVITY 2.2. Job Fair Guidesheet

Purpose: To find out more about various jobs by asking relevant questions during a job fair visit.

Directions:
1. Complete the Introduction section.
2. Review the questions you might ask an employer at a job fair.
3. Role-play a visit to an employer at a job fair. Introduce yourself and ask two or three questions. Thank the person for talking with you.
4. When you visit the job fair, introduce yourself and ask two or three questions of at least three employers.
5. Add this Guidesheet to your Job Notebook.

Introduction
Hello, my name is _____. I am a student at _____.

Questions
- **Can you tell me more about your company?**
- **What training or education is required for a job at your company?**
- **What personal qualities do you look for in your employees?**
- **What do you like best about working for your company?**

Thank you for talking with me.

PERSONAL ASSESSMENT: IDENTIFYING PERSONAL STRENGTHS, INTERESTS, AND CHALLENGES RELATED TO EMPLOYMENT

Individuals on the autism spectrum have much to offer an employer. Though no two individuals on the spectrum are identical, many have traits such as excellent long-term memory, attentiveness to detail, honesty, and loyalty. However, the individual may be unaware of their strengths or how they relate to particular employment opportunities. Challenges in interpreting social cues limit the information the individual with ASD picks up about himself/herself, and they may find it difficult to communicate their strengths appropriately. For example, a student with ASD may respond with "I'm nice and I'm good at video games" when asked, "What are your personal strengths?" In addition, a hyperfocus on a particular area of interest may result in "tunnel vision" when it comes to matching interests with the job market.

As challenging as the task of personal assessment may be, a match between the employee's needs and abilities and the job context is essential. LaRue and colleagues (2019) found that individuals performed better at their jobs when they were in jobs that matched their profile based on a brief, skill-based vocational assessment. Self-assessments, aptitude tests, and interest surveys are useful tools for helping individuals with ASD to identify their strengths and interests. Assessment tools include formal and informal means of identifying strengths and interests. According to Yvona Fast, author of *Employment for Individuals with Asperger Syndrome or Non-Verbal Learning Disability: Stories and Strategies* (2004), it is especially important for the job seeker to know themselves well before entering the job market (Fast, 2012).

Self-assessments, by their nature, illuminate not only strengths but also areas of weakness. Challenges and limitations need to be assessed honestly. The individual should ask not only "Can I overcome this?" but also "Do I *want* to overcome this?" The job seeker needs to know they have no need to prove they do not fit the stereotype of an individual with ASD. Choosing a job that foregrounds an area of weakness generally impedes success—for those with or without a disability. Choosing not to persist in overcoming an area of weakness is not failure but a valid choice, and choosing not to put forth effort in overcoming an area of weakness may, in fact, allow the job seeker to devote more attention to developing areas of strength (Fast, 2012).

Peers and caring adults play a crucial role in helping the individual with ASD to assess their strengths and interests, and to identify potential hurdles in the employment preparation process. However, one of the hardest realities to face as an autistic self-advocate or the parent of an autistic child is that their abilities are not always enough to get—and keep—a good job. For example, a young autistic adult could be a brilliant mathematician, but if they can't generalize their skills to a needed function, such as accounting or statistics, they may not be able to capitalize on their mathematical skill in the job setting. Other issues that can be serious obstacles to employment for autistic adults include

- social anxiety,
- severe sensory challenges,
- inflexibility,
- difficulty handling criticism, and
- unwillingness to share or collaborate.

Autistic adults need to understand—and accept as best they can—their strengths and challenges in the workplace. Once strengths and challenges have been identified, a person can advocate for training, internships, and "job carving" to help the individual with ASD find the best job match.

Appropriate guidance in the job preparation process includes conversations about whether to disclose a disability. Though the job seeker may desire to blend in and not call attention to their disability, research indicates that disclosing often leads to increased chances of employment success. Potential benefits of disclosing include

- protection under ADA,
- better understanding from supervisors and coworkers,
- less chance of being misinterpreted or misunderstood, and
- opportunities to educate others. (Ciampi, 2018)

The MAP and STAR tools described later in this chapter provide avenues for the job seeker's supporters to engage in the process while promoting the individual's sense of agency. In addition, the Underlying Characteristics Checklist (UCC-CL) provides a useful checklist to assess characteristics in the following areas:

- Social
- Patterns of behavior, interests, and activities
- Communication
- Sensory differences
- Cognitive differences
- Motor differences
- Emotional vulnerability
- Medical or biological factors (Aspy & Grossman, 2007)

The checklist can be completed by the individual with ASD, though it is recommended that those who support the individual provide input as well. A sample of the UCC-CL can be found at https://autisminternetmodules.org/storage/ocali-ims-sites/ocali-ims-aim/documents/ElleCaseStudy.pdf.

Activity 2.3 contains many useful resources for career exploration, such as profiles and inventories, and can be found at the O*NET resource center.

ACTIVITY 2.3. Career Exploration and Interest Profiles

Use the O*NET resource center (https://www.onetcenter.org/) to access career exploration information and a variety of online resources and assessments, such as the Interest Profiler and Work Importance Profiler.

A Lifebook such as the sample described in Activity 2.4 is a useful tool for clarifying personal interests and goals. In addition, once completed, the Lifebook can be taken to an interview as a prompt for discussing personal strengths and interests.

ACTIVITY 2.4.   Lifebook or Lifebox

The purpose of a Lifebook (or Lifebox) is to promote self-determination by assembling a scrapbook that showcases an individual's life story. The Lifebook or Lifebox is a collection of artifacts, such as photos, magazine pictures, keepsakes, writings, songs, maps, and hobby memorabilia. The artifacts help to answer these questions:

Who am I?
What is important to me?
Who is important to me?
What interests do I have?
What hopes and dreams do I have?

Pages in a Lifebook might include:

What I love about me
People I am thankful for
Things I love to do
Things I like
Things I dislike
What I want people to know about me
My favorite places
Things most people don't know about me

The Lifebook or Lifebox can be used to help the individual with ASD develop skills in:

Identifying and communicating strengths
Appropriately discussing interests
Self-advocating

(adapted from GatewaytoSD, 2011)

Activity 2.5: Personal Inventory Worksheet

Use the Activity 2.5: Personal Inventory Worksheet to identify strengths, interests, weaknesses, and areas for growth. Then ask for input from others. Do you agree or disagree with the assessment of others? Be sure to supply evidence for agreeing or disagreeing.

ACTIVITY 2.5.   Personal Inventory Worksheet
___

Purpose: To self-assess interests, skills, and abilities.

Directions:
1. Respond to the prompts below.
2. Add this worksheet to your Job Notebook.

Interests and Abilities

When I have free time, my favorite thing to do is _____.

Other things I like to do in my free time include _____
_____.

I prefer to be: alone   with one or two people   with a group

Others say I'm good at _____.

I think I'm good at _____.

Looking Ahead

My dream job is _____.

To be good at that job a person needs to _____
_____.

I think I would be good at my dream job because I _____
_____.

In order to succeed at my dream job, I would need to learn more about _____
_____.

Things that might make it hard for me to get my dream job include: _____
_____.

To overcome the things that are hard for me, I would need to _____
_____.

Some people and resources that could help me overcome the challenges include: _____
_____
_____.

Job seekers with ASD need assurance that their preferences matter. Better matches lead to higher job performance, productivity, satisfaction, and accuracy in tasks. Job preference assessment is a valuable strategy that leads to better employment outcomes (Iacomini et al., 2021). Client choices and preferences for various aspects of a job, such as much or little interaction, repetitive or complex tasks, sedentary or mobile tasks have been shown to improve job success (Hall, 2014, as cited in Iacomini et al., 2021).

ACTIVITY 2.6.   Written Interest Assessment: Coding Interests

Go to the "Written Interest Assessment: Coding Interests" in *Internships: The On-Ramp to Employment*, a publication of the National Consortium on Leadership and Disability for Youth, found at http://www.ncld-youth.info/Downloads/intern-guide-final.pdf.

Identify two areas of interest by following the steps on pages 11–13 of the document. See Table 2.2 for additional preferences that may be considered.

TABLE 2.2.   Job Preferences

Tasks	Environment	Personal
Active or sedentary	Noise levels	Hours:
Physical exertion	Leave policy	Full or part time
Importance of accuracy	Inside or outside	Scheduling: Fixed or changing
Importance of speed	Small or large company	Weekdays/weekends
Manual labor or desk work	Access to food	Pay and benefits
Complex or simple tasks	Distance to and from jobsite;	Training
Novel or repetitive tasks	available transportation	On-the-job support
Clarity of expectations	Fast or slow pace	Much or little interaction with
Detail or big-picture oriented		supervisors and coworkers
		Level and context of interaction
		with the general public
		Expectations for grooming and
		hygiene
		Personal space
		Status
		Autism awareness training

Person-Centered Planning

An individual's career path is shaped by personal interests, abilities, access to education, life experiences, and the support of family and friends. As with other aspects of transition planning, when it comes to preparation for a career, students with ASD should be encouraged to seek input from their family, teachers, and other school personnel, and they should engage with community resources (Buron & Wolfberg, 2014). Most importantly, though, the individual needs to be involved in all phases of the planning. While this may seem obvious, well-meaning family and friends can derail the job preparation process, as well as a developing sense of self-determination, by imposing their preferences on the job seeker.

A person-centered approach to planning aims to ensure that the individual most directly affected by the plan is, in fact, *central*. Though the value of the input of those who know the individual best and who care deeply about the job seeker's welfare cannot be underestimated, the top priority needs to be the things the job seeker considers most important. Overall, the purpose of person-centered career planning is to assess where a student is, focus on strengths and challenges, and develop and prioritize goals for employment, while maximizing the individual's involvement in the process (Buron & Wolfberg, 2014).

Blessing (2001) identifies three components for successful, person-centered planning (PCP) that can be applied to the overall career planning process:

1. *Choice and Advocacy*: Students need to understand the range of career possibilities they can explore, and they need the support of family and others to make choices and self-advocate.
2. *Infusing a Person-Centered Planning Approach into Transition Planning*: Students need opportunities and support to envision their future job options. The student needs to feel that they have a sense of control over the plan.
3. *Opportunities for Individualized, Inclusive Options in School and the Community, and the Resources and Supports to Access Them*: The student needs to feel that his or her career choices are real, and that options, as well as resources, have been provided that suit the needs of the student.

PCP is "a family of approaches for discovering what is most important to a person/group and specifying the opportunities and support required to give them the best chance of experiencing what is most important" (West Sussex County Council, 2017, p. 3). Two useful tools for PCP are MAPs (Making Action Plans; Falvey et al., 2020) and STAR (Students Transitioning to Adult Roles; Hayes & Muldoon, 2013). These planning tools utilize graphic organizers and the support of people who care about the individual to help him or her envision their future.

THE MAPS PROCESS

The focus person can choose who to invite to their MAPs session. An adult helper is designated to record the focus person's key ideas through words (and possibly graphics) on a large sheet of mural paper that has been taped to the wall.

1. The facilitator explains the MAPs purpose, the process, and ground rules for input by supporters.
2. *The Story*: The focus person is invited to share the highlights of their "story" so far. What key events stand out to you in your life? Who are the key people? What are the things that have been important to you?
3. Supporters are invited to add to the focus person's "story," sharing the strengths and gifts they have noticed.
4. *The Dream*: The purpose of the "dream phase" is to help the focus person envision their future. Prompts might include: What is your dream in life? If you could see a "perfect day" for you 10 years from now, what would it look like? What would you like to be doing 10 years from now—something that would really make you happy? Invite the supporters to contribute.
5. *The Nightmare*: The purpose of *recognizing the nightmare* is to identify concerns the focus person has about the future and to help them feel empowered to move toward a future guided by their own choices. Prompts might include: What would you want to avoid at all costs in the future? What would a "nightmare day" for you 10

years from now look like? What would make you feel trapped and powerless? What does the nightmare teach us about what is important to you? In a graphic surrounding the "nightmare," invite supporters to suggest strengths and positive character qualities of the focus person. Explain that these traits "create a wall" that helps to keep the nightmare from happening.

6. *Who is the person and what are they good at?* Invite the supporters to contribute to the graphic by identifying what the focus person contributes to others, how they make a positive difference, and their most special qualities.

7. *What will it take?* What are the person's needs? The focus person and supporters identify the people, resources, events, experiences, and growth areas that will help the focus person move toward the dream and avoid the nightmare. Write out specific action steps.

8. *Commitment:* The focus person and supporters are invited to sign the MAP indicating their ongoing support and encouragement as the focus person moves toward their dream.

THE STAR PROCESS

The STAR Process (Hayes & Muldoon, 2013) is designed for the individual with a disability transitioning to a postsecondary educational program. Student voice is a crucial part of the STAR process. The student is empowered to communicate their vision for what they want their future to look like through meetings with a facilitator and the use of the STAR Chart tool. See Table 2.3 for a summary of the steps in the STAR PCP process.

TABLE 2.3. Summary of Steps in the STAR PCP Process

Team Members	Tasks
Facilitator and Student	Pre-meeting: Explain the STAR PCP process to the student, ensuring that they know they are the "star" of the process.
Facilitator and Parents Facilitator and Student	Pre-meeting interviews with parents and then with the student to determine the degree to which future plans for the student align.
Facilitator, Student, Recorder, and Guests	Meeting: Student serves as host. Facilitator explains the STAR Process and the STAR Chart tool. All team members brainstorm a list of student's "star qualities." Facilitator and student role-play to identify student's vision of his/her future. Facilitator leads a conversation about student's current ability levels in each of the five domains Identify possible action steps for each domain.
Facilitator and Student	Post-meeting: Create a STAR Action Plan with specific goals for the coming year. Monitor progress, adjusting the plan as needed.

Note. From Hayes & Muldoon (2013).

ACTIVITY 2.7: STAR PROCESS

The purposes of the STAR Person-Centered Planning process include

- identify hopes and dreams for the future;
- identify and support the acquisition of necessary skills;
- create an action plan with specific goals, objectives, and sources of support;
- embed flexibility in the plan; and
- encourage the development of lifelong goals and continued growth.

Using the STAR Chart tool:

- *Background*: Student's "star" qualities; What makes the individual special?
- *Center star*: Student's future hopes; a visual reminder that the student is central.
- *Five Arrows*: Represent the five domain clusters from the Project 10 STING RAY Curriculum; record action steps in each domain. (More information about the Project 10 STING RAY Curriculum can be found at http://www.fltpsid.info/DetailPage.php?PageID=68.)

A webinar on the STAR PCP process can be found at http://project10.info/Star.php.

ACTIVITY 2.7. Students Transitioning to Adult Roles (STAR) Chart Tool

Purpose: To facilitate the creation of an action plan based on the individual's future goals and present status in each of the five domains: Career Development and Employment, Academic Enrichment, Community Engagement, Independent Living, and Self-Determination.

Directions:

1. With a facilitator, identify the student's strengths. List these between the arrows of the STAR chart.
2. Support the student in envisioning their future: *"Pretend you and I are meeting five years from now. What job are you doing now? What do you like about it?"* List the job in the center "star" section of the chart.
3. With the facilitator, determine the student's current level in each domain. In the stem of the arrow, write examples of competence in the domain.
4. In the tips of the arrows, write specific action steps to move the student closer to their "star" goal.

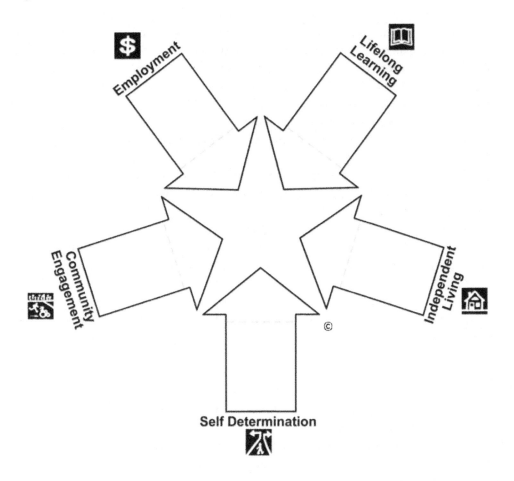

(adapted from Hayes & Muldoon, 2013)

Fostering Self-Determination

A sense of self-determination (i.e., a sense of personal agency in decision making and goal attainment), leads to improved postsecondary outcomes in employment, as well as an improved quality of life (Shogren et al., 2013; Wehmeyer, 2005; Wehmeyer & Palmer, 2003). When students are not only involved in the planning but are central to the planning, they are more likely to gain a sense of self-determination, although, for individuals with ASD, this usually does not occur without intentional guidance from caring adults.

The decision to self-disclose about a disability is an aspect of self-determination that can impact employment success. Dreaver and colleagues (2019) identified understanding by supervisors and coworkers, as well as workplace support, as crucial factors in successful employment for those with ASD. Without self-disclosure, neither would be likely. With support, job seekers with ASD can learn to articulate their strengths, weaknesses, and needs. (See Chapter 7 for a more in-depth discussion of self-disclosure.)

Self-determination requires the cultivation of self-awareness by identifying personal preferences, interests, and challenges, in addition to skills in problem solving and goal attainment. In the process, students need to have the opportunity to take risks, experience failure (preferably in a low-stakes environment), and learn to utilize failures to grow personally and professionally.

Explicit instruction in decision making and problem solving promotes self-determination. Guide students as they break down decision making into steps:

1. Brainstorm a list of possible options. Use your own ideas and the ideas of others.
2. Think about the pros and cons of the options. Write them down and then discuss them with a friend or family member.
3. Choose: Make a choice based on the information at hand.
4. Move forward! No one makes perfect decisions all the time. Poor decisions provide opportunities to learn from mistakes and make better decisions in the future.

Role-play is a good tool for teaching decision making and problem solving. Provide students with scenarios, provide prompts and feedback, and give multiple opportunities to practice decision-making and problem-solving skills in a low-risk environment.

Goal Setting

Identifying a goal is the first phase of the process of goal attainment, but it can be a challenging one for the young adult with ASD. Dean and colleagues (2019) argue that because those on the spectrum often lack the experiences of neurotypical youth, such as extracurricular classes, part-time jobs, and volunteer opportunities, the goal-setting and problem-solving abilities of the job seeker with ASD can be vastly improved through participation in such experiences. Job shadowing, school-based work experiences, internships, and volunteer opportunities can help the job seeker to clarify goals for future employment, as well as identify some of the challenges that need to be overcome to succeed in the job market.

In addition to prioritizing the job seeker's sense of what is important, a good plan begins at the end. What is the job seeker's primary goal? To have a job that supports an independent living arrangement? To work in an area of particular interest—a "dream job"? The job seeker's goal shapes the plan and informs short-term goals that make the path to the primary goal clear and attainable. Executive functioning impairment can complicate the ability to see how parts of a plan figure into the big picture. In addition, planning and prioritizing the steps necessary to make a goal a reality can be challenging. Therefore, the individual with ASD benefits from support in setting goals based on self-assessment. The following are some questions parents, teachers, and community members can ask to help job seekers set realistic goals (Buron & Wolfberg, 2008).

1. What activities or interests do you have?
2. What do you dislike doing?
3. What are you really good at?
4. What do you know a lot about?
5. What do you want to be doing 10 years from now? Why? How badly do you want to do it?
6. Why do you think you would be good at doing that?
7. What support would you need?
8. Who can help you achieve your dream?

In order to be useful, goals need to be specific and actionable. In other words, will the person know if the goal has been attained? If so, it is specific enough. Can the goal be attained by reasonable steps? If so, the goal is actionable. Specific, actionable goals related to future employment can be set in the following areas (Morningstar & Clavenna-Deane, 2018):

- Academic
- Job-related skills and training
- Behavior
- Relationships
- Social skills

Once job seekers identify realistic goals, they need to identify the action steps and know how to adjust the plan if it doesn't work. Below are some things to consider when setting goals related to employment (adapted from Fast, 2004).

- What is the overarching goal?
  - Is the goal specific?
  - Can the goal be reached by following particular steps?
- How much do I care about achieving this goal?
- If I do not achieve this goal, what outcomes are likely? What other options could be considered?
- What "mini-goals" do I need to set in order to achieve this goal?
  - Education/Training

- ° Development of personal qualities
- ° Development of social skills
- ° Development of communication skills
- ° Career research
- What action steps should I take to achieve each goal? In what order should I do them?
- How long will it take to achieve each goal?
- What challenges am I likely to encounter as I aim to meet my goals?
- What sources of support (people and other resources) can help me to meet my goals?

ACTIVITY 2.8: SETTING GOOD GOALS

Use Activity 2.8 to set specific, actionable goals.

ACTIVITY 2.8.   Setting Good Goals

Purpose: To articulate goals and identify actionable steps to achieve the goals.

Directions:
1. Identify three to five goals. The goals should be specific and actionable. *(Will you know you have accomplished it?)*
2. For each goal, identify at least one action step you need to take in order to achieve the goal.
3. Set a target date for completing each action step.
4. Write the date in the box when an action step is completed.
5. Keep these pages in your Job Notebook.

My goal is to _____.
(What do you want to learn, do, or get?)

This is important to me because _____.

So, I will need to:

Action Step	Target Date	Completion Date

My goal is to _____.
(What do you want to learn, do, or get?)

This is important to me because _____.

So, I will need to:

Action Step	Target Date	Completion Date

My goal is to _____.

(What do you want to learn, do, or get?)

This is important to me because _____ .

So, I will need to: _____

Action Step	Target Date	Completion Date

My goal is to _____ .
(What do you want to learn, do, or get?)

This is important to me because _____ .

So, I will need to: _____

Action Step	Target Date	Completion Date

My goal is to _____ .
(What do you want to learn, do, or get?)

This is important to me because _____ .

So, I will need to: _____

Action Step	Target Date	Completion Date

(Adapted from Institute for Educational Leadership, 2018)

How to Help When the Job Seeker Is Stuck

A tendency to perseverate can cause the job seeker with ASD to get stuck on a particular dream, one that may be out of reach. Individuals with ASD benefit from caring adults who encourage them to persevere while also helping them to be realistic.

Here are some tips to help the job seeker move forward (Bernick & Holden, 2015):

1. Don't avoid having the conversation.
2. Avoid giving advice—telling them what to do. Rather, ask questions: Tell me about what you'd like to do. How can I help you with your job search? I understand why you might want to____, but have you considered these challenges? Have you considered a similar path that might be more manageable, especially in the short term?
3. Offer support, such as gathering career information, arranging workplace visits, or helping to develop areas of challenge.

CAREER EXPLORATION

Exploring Job Demands

Internet job boards are an excellent tool for learning about the variety of jobs available. Job seekers can learn about job descriptions, qualifications, expectations, and salary. Sites like Indeed.com, Monster.com, or FlexJobs can be rich sources of exploration. In addition, Career One Stop (https://www.careeronestop.org/) features hundreds of videos of people performing various jobs. The videos serve as springboards for discussion about the demands of the jobs and the qualifications that would be needed. Other sources of exploration include

- mentorships,
- job shadowing,
- classes,
- career research,
- interviews,
- school-based work experiences, and
- volunteer work. (Morningstar et al., 2012)

ACTIVITY 2.9: JOB ANALYSIS WORKSHEET

See Activity 2.9 for a job analysis worksheet. Compare the qualifications and demands of the job with the job seeker's strengths and abilities. What steps would need to be taken in order to prepare for this job? (Consider job training/education, strengths, weaknesses, and preferences.)

ACTIVITY 2.9. Job Analysis Worksheet

Purpose: To assess the match between a job seeker and a job.

Directions:
1. Go to a job board site, like Monster.com, Indeed.com, or FlexJobs.
2. Search for a job you think you may be qualified for.
3. List the qualifications for three job postings.
4. Put a checkmark in the boxes of the qualifications you meet.
5. For qualifications you do not meet, what would you need to learn or do?

Qualifications for Job 1   *I meet the qualification.*

_____

_____

_____

_____

_____

_____
_____
_____
_____

Qualifications for Job 2   *I meet the qualification.*

_____
_____
_____
_____
_____
_____
_____
_____
_____

Qualifications for Job 3   *I meet the qualification.*

_____
_____
_____
_____
_____
_____
_____
_____
_____

For Job 1, I would need to _____. I would/would not want to do this.
For Job 2, I would need to _____. I would/would not want to do this.
For Job 3, I would need to _____. I would/would not want to do this.

Finding a Match

Assessing the match appropriately is a critical factor in long-term job success (Mawhood & Howlin, 1999). Job matching involves identifying strengths, weaknesses, and a plan for overcoming weaknesses (Morgan, 2008, as cited in Iacomini et al., 2021), as well as matching job demands with personal preferences.

Being qualified doesn't mean it's a good match. For example, being good at computers doesn't mean a person would be good as a helpdesk employee if that person gets nervous talking to people. According to the Autism Society (2019), job seekers with ASD should limit their search to jobs that require minimal social interaction and that have clear goals or endpoints. There's no one-size-fits-all job that's great for those with ASD, but it is best to avoid jobs that emphasize weaknesses in favor of those that focus on strengths and match the job seeker's profile. The University of Indiana's Autistic Job Recommendations can help job seekers identify a good match: https://www.iidc.indiana.edu/irca/articles/choosing-the-right-job-for-people-with-autism-or-aspergers-syndrome.html.

It's important to find a job that matches the individual's interests, abilities, and strengths. Hendricks (2010) found that employees with ASD performed at levels equal to or superior to neurotypical coworkers when the job was matched correctly to their interests, preferences, and abilities. Not only does the individual's sense of self-worth increase, but so does job satisfaction. It's important that we assist the individual with ASD in recognizing these strengths and interests and provide them with ways to demonstrate and articulate them in the job interview. Additionally, we need to analyze the skills and abilities required for the job and ensure a match with the individual's skills and abilities. Both physical (endurance, fine motor ability) and mental (concentration, working alone) abilities and preferences should be considered in the job-matching process.

To help identify a job you are interested in, as well as well suited for, use the "Favorite Jobs Matrix" from *What Color Is Your Parachute? 2017: A Practical Manual for Job-Hunters and Career-Changers* by R. N. Bolles (2017, p. 176).

SUMMARY

This chapter guides the practitioner as they help job seekers take a realistic look at their skills and abilities and the demands of various jobs. There's no one-size-fits-all job for individuals with ASD, but finding a match between employer and employment is crucial for a successful job experience. This chapter provides an overview of the job search, tools for self-assessment, and guidance for setting realistic employment goals.

ADDITIONAL RESOURCES

- Self-determination framework: https://www.aucd.org/docs/Advising-Through-SD.pdf
- MAPs and PATH: For detailed instructions, examples, and videos, see
  - https://schools.local-offer.org/childs-journey/paths-bella/ (Facilitator's Guide)
  - https://westsussex.local-offer.org/information_pages/128-person-centred-planning-pcp-path-training-videos
  - https://westsussex.local-offer.org/information_pages/388-person-centred-planning-pcp-map-training-videos
- Autism-friendly employers:
  - https://www.verywellhealth.com/top-autism-friendly-employers-4159784
  - https://www.verywellhealth.com/things-you-need-to-know-about-autism-and-employment-4159850#citation-7

- Speech and communication: https://www.verywellhealth.com/speech-vs-communication-260566
- To disclose or not to disclose: https://researchautism.org/disclosing-autism-on-the-job-yes-or-no/
- Job-matching quiz (UK based): https://www.prospects.ac.uk/careers-advice/getting-a-job
- Employment resources: https://autismsociety.org/resources/employment/
- Career exploration, assessments, and profiles:
  - O*NET Resource Center, www.onetcenter.org
  - Career One Stop, https://www.careeronestop.org/
- Interest Assessment and other resources for internships: https://geneticalliance.org/pdf/advocacy-atlas/education-services/intern-guide-final.pdf
- Project 10 STING RAY Curriculum for Transition (STAR Process): http://project10.info/files/P10STINGRAYBrochure.pdf
- Job Recommendations for Individuals with Autism: https://www.iidc.indiana.edu/irca/articles/choosing-the-right-job-for-people-with-autism-or-aspergers-syndrome.html

CHAPTER 3

Beginning the Job Application Process

∙∙∙

Teacher: What skills can you list on your résumé?
Student: Well, I'm really good at video games.

THINGS TO THINK ABOUT

- How might ASD complicate the process of preparing job applications and résumés?
- In what ways might the individual with ASD be at a disadvantage in the competitive employment market?

Applying for a job can quickly prove discouraging for individuals on the spectrum, simply because the job seekers' areas of greatest challenge are often foregrounded throughout the process. Discussing strengths appropriately, seeing things from the perspective of another person, and understanding the confusing terminology of job applications are just a few of the ways autism can complicate the process of applying for a job. This chapter includes resources and activities to help the job seeker with ASD consider what an employer needs to know and how to communicate this information effectively through job applications and a well-developed résumé. Job Notebook activities will help the prospective employee begin to develop a résumé and to interpret and complete various types of job applications.

THE CHALLENGES: PERSPECTIVES OF POTENTIAL EMPLOYERS

As employers seek to staff their organization with the employee who is the best match for a position, they often weed through multiple applications and résumés. The employer tries to determine which candidate has not only the skills needed to perform the job effectively, but, sometimes equally importantly: Who will be the best fit with the existing employees? Assessing a candidate's skills, training, and experience is merely the first step in the selection process. Employers often have multiple candidates for one position, and the job application and résumé are often an employer's first contact with a

∙∙∙

candidate. Therefore, the job application and résumé are essential to making a positive first impression.

As mentioned in the previous chapter, some corporations actively seek out individuals with disabilities, and this trend seems to be on the rise. While the Americans with Disabilities Act (ADA) protects individuals with disabilities from discrimination (U.S. Department of Labor, n.d.b.), hiring employees with disabilities benefits employers in many ways. Employees with disabilities may bring alternative perspectives, including insights into the needs of customers with disabilities, high productivity, loyalty and long-term job retention, and tax incentives (DO-IT, 2022).

However, in the competitive job market, the job seeker with ASD is often at a disadvantage from the start. Because of a tendency to have interests that are narrow and deep, rather than broad, as well as a variety of social challenges, individuals on the spectrum may have a more limited background of experience than their neurotypical peers. They may have limited educational achievements and a minimal or nonexistent work history. In addition, employers are often reluctant to hire individuals with ASD due to stereotyped perceptions and misinformation (Solomon, 2020). Employers may erroneously believe that hiring employees with ASD is not cost-effective, that the employee will be incapable of the tasks, or that they will require too much support.

PAVING THE WAY: NETWORKING

Referring to the traditional means of seeking employment by submitting an application and/or résumé through a job board, job coach Cindy Zoeller (as quoted in Bernick & Holden, 2015, p. 104) says of job seekers with ASD, "to stand out enough to be selected for an interview—solely off of an application and a résumé . . . hasn't happened in my experience." Though this is a bleak perspective, and one that may not apply to the young adult applying for lower-level jobs, the challenges for the job seeker on the spectrum cannot be underestimated. Communication deficits, including difficulty identifying and articulating strengths appropriately, as well as social skills deficits that may limit the background of experience an applicant brings to the job setting, can keep the application of an individual with ASD from rising to the top of the applicant pool.

According to Cornell University's Career Services, networking plays a role in many hiring decisions. In fact, as many as 80% of jobs never get posted (U.S. Department of Labor, n.d.d.). Rather than taking a risk on candidates who may turn out to be quite different on the job than they appeared during the hiring process, employers often prefer to hire based on the recommendations of current employees and others whose opinions they know and trust.

For the job seeker with ASD, networking can be a crucial means of paving the way to employment, one that should be maximized. Because many individuals with ASD tend to be shy (Kim, 2014), and have communication and social skills deficits, the idea of networking can prove more than a little intimidating. Understanding what networking is and how to develop and maintain a network are integral to the job-search process.

First, what is *networking*? A network is a group of people with whom you interact. In *Soft Skills to Pay the Bills* (U.S. Department of Labor, n.d.d.), a personal network is differentiated from a professional network. A personal network includes family, friends, acquaintances, teachers, coworkers, fellow parishioners, and others with whom a person interacts regularly for the purpose of sharing information and experiences. A professional network may include some of the same people, but the purpose differs. The purpose of a professional network is to meet and expand career goals. A network should never be a one-way street. As part of a network, whether personal or professional, a person should aim to contribute to others, even as they benefit from the connections.

Shyness, a lack of confidence, difficulty communicating, and difficulty reading social cues can complicate networking for the individual with ASD, but every person can learn to improve their networking skills—an essential step, given the percentage of jobs acquired through networking and the increased challenges to employment experienced by those on the spectrum. Job seekers can begin to develop their network by identifying the people who are currently in it.

Activity 3.1: Spheres of Influence

Use the worksheet in Activity 3.1 (adapted from U.S. Department of Labor, n.d.d., Activity 20) to identify the people currently in your network. How many people do you know who may be able to help spread the word of your job search? Next, look at each person in your network. Consider that each person in your network probably has as many contacts as you do. Multiply the number of people in your network by that same number. How many potential connections does your network help to facilitate?

After identifying the individuals in a person's network, the next step is to talk with people in the network and ask them to help spread the word about the job search. Articulating career goals, strengths, and skills appropriately can be challenging for the individual with ASD for many reasons. Shyness, as well as some of the challenges addressed in the previous chapter, such as difficulty articulating strengths and skills in an appropriate way, can complicate networking. Lara Zielin (2012), author of *Make Things Happen: The Key to Networking for Teens*, proposes "the three Ps of networking:" prepare, practice, and "pull yourself together." The nervous job seeker can *prepare* by writing out what they will say and *practice* by rehearsing with a friend. Good grooming and appropriate dress contribute to a sense of confidence that can help the job seeker *pull themselves together*. Also, the nervous job seeker should engage in positive self-talk. Here are a few prompts:

- I have valuable abilities to offer an employer.
- I am taking an important step toward achieving my goals.
- Feeling nervous is normal, but I will take control to accomplish my goals.

Because the individual with ASD may not have the broad range of social contacts that result from typical youth activities like clubs, scouting, music lessons, internships, and summer jobs, they may benefit from intentional opportunities to build a network by engaging with those who can facilitate a career path.

ACTIVITY 3.1. Spheres of Influence

Purpose: To identify people in your network who can help to spread the word about your job search.

Directions:
1. In the center white circle, list the names of people who are closest to you. "Center circle people" are those you care deeply about and you see often. Parents, grandparents, brothers and sisters, and best friends might be in this category.
2. In the second white circle, list the names of people that you know and come into contact with on a regular or somewhat regular basis but that you don't have a close relationship with. Students in your gym class, coworkers, teachers, relatives in your extended family, counselors, and friends of your parents might be in this category.
3. Count all of the people you have listed in both circles.
4. Multiply the number of people in your circles by that number. So, for example, if you have 10 people in your circles, multiply 10 x 10, which equals 100. This is the number of potential connections you have.
5. Add this page to your Job Notebook.

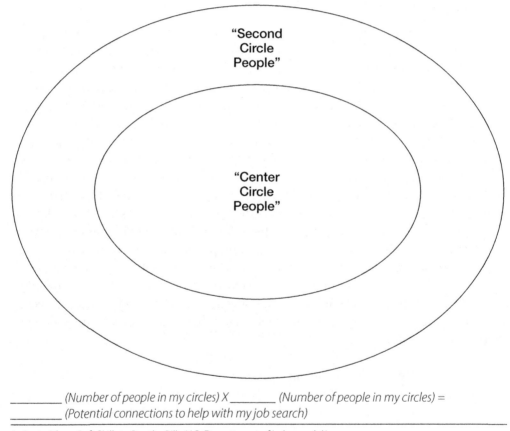

_____ (Number of people in my circles) X _____ (Number of people in my circles) =
_____ (Potential connections to help with my job search)

(adapted from Soft Skills to Pay the Bills, U.S. Department of Labor, n.d.d.)

Here are some possibilities:

- Job fairs
- Guest speakers
- Volunteer work
- Social media
- Informational interviews (more about this in Chapter 4)
- Family and friends (never underestimate this one!)

Help job seekers to network effectively by engaging in the three Ps prior to the networking opportunity. Brainstorm appropriate ways to *prepare* for the opportunity, such as generating a list of questions or researching a career, a specific company, or an individual.

Practice by role-playing interactions in dyads or teams. Discuss and model good grooming and hygiene practices, as well as appropriate dress for various contexts, to help the networker *pull it together* and make the most of the opportunity. Finally, follow up with a thank-you note whenever someone gives of their time and attention to support the job seeker.

Social media offers the potential for a personal or professional network to expand exponentially, and job seekers on the spectrum may find communication much easier through a social media platform than face to face. Unlike real-time conversation, social media users can take their time to think about what they want to say, try out different ways to word a message, or solicit feedback from a friend or family member prior to going public with a message or a question. In addition, fidgeting and physical tics that may increase with stress won't distract from the interaction.

Encourage job seekers to create a LinkedIn profile. Bernick and Holden (2015) caution against *not* having a LinkedIn profile. Though an individual with ASD may not secure a job offer through LinkedIn, not having a LinkedIn profile available may raise a red flag to potential employers, prompting them to disregard the application.

Informing online contacts about the job search can open up additional possibilities, but this should be done with care and professionalism. (More about professionalism later.) Since a person's online "footprint" can negatively impact the job search process, job seekers should search for themselves to see what kind of an impression their online presence suggests to a potential employer. According to CareerBuilder.com (as referenced in U.S. Department of Labor, n.d.d.), job seekers should be especially careful about what they post, make information and posts "private" when possible, and check their profile frequently. LinkedIn can be a good way to enhance an applicant's online presence.

ACTIVITY 3.2. Preparing for Networking Opportunities

Purpose: To prepare for interactions with guest speakers or at job fairs.

First, consider how you will introduce yourself.

Hello, my name is _____.

I am a _____ at _____.

    (Say something about yourself, such as "I am a junior at Rothrock High School.")

I am interested in a job as a _____.

Next, think about questions to ask.

Can you tell me more about your company?

What is your favorite part of your job?

What skills do you look for in your employees?

Add your own questions here:

Things I learned about _____. (Name the company.)

Add this to your Job Notebook!

WRITTEN COMMUNICATION

The Right Kind of Writing for the Right Purpose

Communication skills, particularly nonverbal communication skills, play an important role in the job search process. However, communication challenges among those on the spectrum are many and varied. Failure to pick up on nonverbal social cues often leads to inappropriate interactions, particularly in the professional setting, which may be unfamiliar to the first-time job seeker. The job application process primarily requires written communication, which can be less stressful for some. However, the job seeker with ASD may need explicit instruction in the differences between formal and informal written interactions, including the differences in purpose and style among text messages, email, and letters (see Table 3.1). A template for formal email is included in Activity 3.3.

Any written communication between the applicant and their prospective employer should be formal, at least initially. (See Activity 3.4 for an exercise on differentiating between formal and informal writing.) All written documents should be carefully proofread and free from errors.

TABLE 3.1. Characteristics of Formal and Informal Written Communication

Area of Difference	Formal Written Communication (Business letters, some emails)	Informal Written Communication (Text messages, some emails, friendly letters)
Knowledge of the Recipient	Often minimal or known only in a formal setting	Personal knowledge of the recipient
Greeting and Closing	Formal salutation; may use the person's surname (Dear Ms. _____; To whom it may concern) Formal Closing (Sincerely, Respectfully)	Informal or may be missing (Hey there; see you later)
Focus	Succinct and to the point	May be "chatty" or designed simply to maintain a connection; may have multiple purposes or an unclear purpose
Content	Only content that is relevant to the purpose; stated clearly	May include jokes or sarcasm
Language	Formal language; no slang or unfamiliar abbreviations; longer, more complex sentences	Conversational language; slang; shorter, simpler sentences
Tone	Straightforward and professional; no emoticons	The personality of the writer may come through in the tone of the writing; emoticons can also be used to communicate tone
Format	Follows conventional format for the type of communication (business letter; email with subject line); traditional font and type size, such as 12-point Times New Roman	Format may be defined by the time and space of the writing; may be handwritten or composed on an electronic device; font may reflect the personality of the writer or the topic of the communication
Shared Knowledge	Sender and recipient may not know one another so assumptions are made with caution	Because sender and recipient know one another, information may be missing due to shared understandings and experiences
Position	Often a vertical relationship, with sender or recipient being in a more powerful position than the other	Peer-to-peer
Editing	Carefully proofread with no grammatical or other errors; only conventional spellings are used, with no misspellings	May include unconventional spellings; sometimes contains misspelled words and nonstandard grammar

ACTIVITY 3.3. Email Template

Purpose: To learn to write formal emails.

Directions:
1. Review the parts of a formal email.
2. Use the template to compose a formal email.

Email

The parts of an email include the recipient's email address, the subject line, greeting, body, and signature. Sometimes files are included as "attachments."

Recipient's Email Address: Be sure you type the email address of the recipient accurately and double-check it. If any part of the address is incorrect, the recipient will not receive the email.

Subject Line: Add a subject line (usually between three and eight words) that will help the receiver to know at a glance what the email refers to. Example: Résumé for Cashier Position Attached

Greeting: If you know the recipient's name, you can write, "Dear _____" or just use their name followed by a comma. Check the spelling of the person's name. If you don't know the name, you can begin your email with "Hello." (Avoid informal expressions like "Hey, there!")

Body: State the purpose of your email and provide any necessary information as succinctly as possible.

Signature: Use a closing, such as "sincerely," "respectfully," or "best." Write your first and last name and your complete contact information, including mailing address, phone number, and email address.

Email Template

Recipient's Email Address:

Subject Line:

Hello _____,

Thank you for meeting with me at _____. I enjoyed learning more about your company. As you requested, I am attaching my résumé to this email.

Best,
Name
Mailing address
Cell phone
Email address

ACTIVITY 3.4. Distinguishing Between Formal and Informal Writing

Purpose: To distinguish between formal and informal writing in order to respond to potential employers professionally.

Directions:

1. Read each sample aloud. Some of the samples are just parts of a message, so focus on the part provided.
2. Does the message sound like something you would say to a friend who knows you well? If so, the writing is probably "informal," and would not be an appropriate way to respond to a potential employer. Circle the things that suggest to you that the writing is informal. Put an X on these samples. Check yourself with the answer key.
3. Reread the samples that are not marked with an X. Use these as models for your own correspondence with potential employers.
4. Add this to your Job Notebook.

Sample 1:
Hey there!
How's it going? Not so great here. Jessie's been in the hosital for over a week. Not sure if we're going to be able to come over for the party.

Sample 2:
To whom it may concern:
I am writing to apply for the position of cashier that was advertised on Indeed.com. I am a reliable worker, and I am excellent at handling money. I have attached my résumé. If you think my qualifications match the position, I would be glad for the opportunity to meet with you for an interview.

Sincerely,

Jane Shoop
555 Smith Court
Newtown, NJ 55555
(555) 555-1212
jshoop@gmail.com

Sample 3:
Dear Ms. Donley,
Thank you for meeting with me today about the position of stock clerk. I was glad for the opportunity to learn more about your company and the position. I will bring my paperwork to your office tomorrow, as you requested. If you need anything else, please contact me at: (555) 555-5555 or jmartinez@gmail.com.

Regards,
Joseph Martinez
555 Smith Court
Newtown, NJ 55555
(555) 555-1212
jmartinez@gmail.com

Sample 4:
BTW did you get the math? IDK what we're supp to do ☺

Answer Key:

Sample 1: Informal
The greeting is one you would use for a friend. The sender and recipient have shared knowledge about who "Jessie" is and about the party to be held. Sentences are short. "Hospital" is misspelled.

Sample 2: Formal
The greeting and closing are formal. Sentences are varied and some sentences are long. The message is focused with no extra information. The sender includes all contact information.

Sample 3: Formal
The purpose of the message is clear with no extra information. The tone is polite and respectful. The greeting and closing are formal. All contact information is given. The sender does not assume that the recipient remembers him, so he includes a reminder of their meeting.

Sample 4: Informal
The sender and recipient know each other because no greeting or closing is needed. The sender uses abbreviations that the recipient will understand. They have shared knowledge about a math assignment. Emoticons are used.

Keeping Things Relevant

Weaknesses in theory of mind, that is, "the ability to recognize and understand other people's thoughts, feelings, desires, and intentions in order to make sense of their behavior" (Buron & Wolfberg, 2014, p. 459), complicates the ability to see things from the perspective of an employer. Therefore, the individual with ASD may have difficulty discerning relevant information from the irrelevant when engaging in the job application process.

Prior to the interview (during which the employer will evaluate the prospective employee's "soft skills"), the employer begins to assess the potential employee's fit for the position by examining the applicant's eligibility for employment, relevant training and experiences, and credibility. Both the job application and the résumé include sections that help the employer to determine if the applicant has the necessary qualifications.

In addition to the information provided on the application or résumé, the employer begins to make inferences about the applicant's suitability for the job. For this reason, all contact with the potential employer and staff needs to be courteous and professional. Aspects of professionalism that can sometimes be problematic for individuals on the spectrum, but which employers consider important prior to employment include time management (Solomon, 2020), appropriate social competence and self-confidence (Solomon, 2020), personal care (Dreaver et al., 2019), and business writing (Dreaver et al., 2019).

Though many job applications are completed online, if the applicant stops by a place of employment for a paper application, all interactions—even parking in an appropriate spot—need to be considered part of the job application process. Things to consider for preliminary, in-person visits to a company include

- grooming and hygiene;
- appropriate dress;
- parking;
- greeting staff and customers appropriately;
- being respectful of working staff members' time;
- waiting patiently without interrupting; and
- polite speech, including "please" and "thank you."

Some employers provide paper applications that can be picked up at the place of employment. Role-playing the process of requesting an application in person, as in Activity 3.5, helps the applicant to prepare for this initial contact with the potential employer.

ACTIVITY 3.5.   Role-Play Picking Up an Application in Person

Although most applications are accessed and completed online, some employers prefer that applicants pick up an application in person. Role-play the request for an application, including consideration of the following:

- Locating the appropriate person (consider the employees in a particular workplace setting who would be best suited to help, such as a receptionist)
- Waiting patiently if the person is busy
- Introducing oneself
- Stating the purpose (to pick up a job application)
- Making eye contact
- Shaking hands (only if initiated by the staff person)
- Saying "please" and "thank you"
- Respecting personal space
- Asking for clarification about the employer's preference for the return of the application
- Behaving professionally from the time an applicant arrives in the parking lot until they leave

DEVELOPING A RÉSUMÉ

A résumé is often a potential employer's first impression of the applicant's suitability for the job. The résumé not only showcases the skills and abilities of the applicant, but it also reflects an applicant's writing ability, attention to detail, work ethic, professionalism, and time management skills. The résumé helps to answer the question: Does this applicant have the qualifications for the job?

Though many jobs pursued by first-time job seekers require an application rather than a résumé, developing a résumé first can take some of the mystery out of the job application. Also, because essential information like the correct spelling of names, accurate dates, and addresses are included, the résumé can serve as a "cheat sheet" when completing a job application.

First-time job seekers should aim to compose a basic résumé, but consider it a "living" document. Expect to tweak it for each potential employer, including qualifications specified in the job posting, as appropriate. Also, the document should be updated as the applicant gains further training and experience.

The Basic Résumé

Job seekers should collect the following information to complete a basic résumé. Be sure spellings, names, and dates are accurate. Sections of the résumé are explained here with teacher prompts to help job seekers to identify the correct information.

1. *Contact information:* Contact information enables the employer to contact the applicant for more information or to schedule an interview. Contact information should appear at the top of the résumé.

First and last name

Mailing address: What information is included on letters you receive in the mail? Does it come to your house? If so, the mailing address is usually a house number and the name of the street, city, state, and zip code. If you receive mail at a post office, the address is usually a post office (P.O.) box number, followed by the city, state, and zip code.

Phone number: A personal cell phone number is best. However, be sure to answer all calls professionally once you have applied for a job.

Email address: An email address should be the applicant's name or a variation of the name using initials. Avoid nicknames and references to hobbies, pets, or personality traits in the email address; this can make an applicant appear unprofessional.

ACTIVITY 3.6: RÉSUMÉ CONTACT INFORMATION

Complete the Contact Information worksheet and checklist.

ACTIVITY 3.6.   Résumé Contact Information

Purpose: To accurately include all of the information an employer would need to contact a prospective employee.

Directions:
1. Complete the information on the form.
2. Check with a family member or teacher to be sure you have the correct information.
3. Use the checklist to be sure your contact information is accurate.
4. Add this to your Job Notebook.

Name: _____
(first name; middle initial or name if used; last name)

Mailing address: (Where do you receive your mail?)

Street address: _____

City or town: _____State:_____
(Use the correct two-letter abbreviation)

Zip code: _____ *(The zip code should have five digits.)*

Phone number: _____
Include the three-digit area code and seven-digit phone number, like this: (XXX) XXX-XXXX

Email address: _____ *(Are you using an email address that is professional? No hobbies, nicknames, or personality traits! Double-check for accuracy.)*

Checklist:
_____ Have you included your first name, a middle initial or name if you use it, and last name?
_____ Is the address the one where you receive your mail?
_____ Have you included a street name and number or a post office box number?
_____ Have you spelled your city or town correctly?
_____ Did you use the correct two-letter abbreviation for your state? Did you use two capital letters?
_____ Did you include a five-digit zip code?
_____ Did you include the area code and phone number of a phone that you can answer most of the time?
_____ Is your email address correct?
_____ Is your email address professional?

2. *Objective:* State the position being applied for. (This should be changed to fit the job being applied for.)

ACTIVITY 3.7: "AM I QUALIFIED?"

Using an online job board (e.g., Monster, Indeed, FlexJobs), identify three jobs that you meet the minimum qualifications for. Use the "Am I Qualified?" check sheet in Activity 3.7 to determine whether you meet the qualifications. If you do not meet the qualifications, go to another job posting. Then write an objective statement for each job, using the format:

"Objective: To obtain a position as a _____(position) at _____(company)."

ACTIVITY 3.7.   "Am I Qualified?"

Purpose: To determine whether an applicant meets the minimum qualifications for a particular job.

Directions:
1. Go to an online job board, such as Indeed.com or Monster.com.
2. Put in a search term for a job you think you may be qualified for, such as "cashier" or "stock clerk."
3. Select a job and read the qualifications.
4. When you find a job you meet all qualifications for, list the qualifications.
5. Place a check mark next to each qualification you meet to be sure you really are qualified.
6. If you do not meet even one of the qualifications, go to another job posting and start again. If you find that you are not meeting the qualifications for most jobs, you may need to switch to a different type of job.
7. Find three job postings that you meet all qualifications for.
8. Write an objective statement for each job, using the prompt.
9. Add this to your Job Notebook.

Job 1:
(List the position here.)

What are the qualifications? List them in this column.	Place a check mark in this column if you meet the qualification.

Objective: To obtain a position as a _____ (position) at _____ (company).

Job 2:
(List the position here.)

What are the qualifications? List them in this column.	Place a check mark in this column if you meet the qualification.

Objective: To obtain a position as a _____ *(position)*
at _____ *(company)*.

Job 3:
(List the position here.)

What are the qualifications? List them in this column.	Place a check mark in this column if you meet the qualification.

Objective: To obtain a position as a _____ *(position)*
at _____ *(company)*.

3. *Relevant Experiences:* What experiences have you had that will help you to succeed in the job you are applying for? For example, if you are applying to work as a day care assistant, babysitting or assisting in a Sunday School class would be relevant experiences, because you would be using similar skills in both settings; however, experience with video gaming would not. During the early phases of your career, all part-time and full-time jobs, internships, and many volunteer and job-shadowing opportunities are considered relevant because they provide you with valuable experiences in a work setting. Experiences such as these suggest that you have time management skills and a good work ethic. For each experience listed, include your position (e.g., "cashier"); the employer with the employer's complete address; and dates employed (start to finish). List any of the following in order from most recent to least recent:

- Full- or part-time jobs
- Volunteer work
- Internships
- Job shadowing

ACTIVITY 3.8: RELEVANT EXPERIENCES

Use the Activity 3.8: Relevant Experiences worksheet to identify three experiences that you may want to list on your résumé.

ACTIVITY 3.8.   Relevant Experiences

Purpose: To list experiences that may be relevant to particular jobs.

Directions:
1. List all part-time and full-time jobs, volunteer work, internships, and job-shadowing opportunities.
2. For each experience, list your responsibilities, the employer's name or the company and address, and the dates of the experience.
3. Explain how the experience may help you in another job.
4. Add this to your Job Notebook.

Experiences: Part-time or full-time jobs, volunteer work, internships, job shadowing	Your responsibilities in the experience: What did you do?	Your employer's name or the name of the company and their complete address	The dates of the experience (Example: 9/1/23–5/1/24)	How might the experience help you in another job? What did you learn from the experience? (Include hard skills and soft skills.)

4. **Education and Training:** Beginning with the highest level and the most recent accomplishment, list the high school and any colleges you have attended, as well as any training programs you have completed. If you are currently in high school, list the high school you are attending and list the month and year you expect to graduate. Do not list elementary or middle schools. Include

- school name, city, and state;
- program and degree (colleges only); and
- years attended.

ACTIVITY 3.9: EDUCATION AND TRAINING

Use the Activity 3.9: Education and Training worksheet to list information about your education history.

ACTIVITY 3.9. Education and Training

Purpose: To list all education and trainings you have attended or completed.

Directions:
1. List your high school, the address of the school, and the dates you attended.
2. List any trainings or college you have attended, such as "Red Cross First Aid Training" or "Sunbury College." Include the address of the school and the dates you attended.
3. List any credentials you received for completing a program, such as a diploma, a certificate, or a degree.
4. Add this to your Job Notebook.

School or Training	School Address (City and State)	Dates you attended (Example: 9/1/22–5/1/23). If you don't know the day, just include the months and years	Did you complete the program? If so, list the credential you received: diploma, certificate, or degree

5. **Skills and Abilities:** Think of "skills" as "hard skills," like proficiency with a particular form of technology; specify your level of proficiency, such as "beginner," "proficient," or "advanced." Table 3.2 can help to determine the level of proficiency for entry-level job skill areas.

TABLE 3.2. Skill Proficiency Levels

Skills	Beginner	Proficient	Advanced
Basic Math Skills	I am good at counting, categorizing, adding, and subtracting.	I am good at counting, categorizing, adding, subtracting, multiplying, and dividing. I can use math tools, such as a calculator, effectively. I can catch and correct my own mistakes.	I am good at adding, subtracting, multiplying, and dividing. I can calculate percentages and fractions. I use math tools, such as a calculator, effectively. I rarely make mistakes in math.
Spelling and Grammar	I spell most words correctly, and I can use spell-check effectively. When writing, I correctly use simple sentence structures.	I rarely misspell words, and I can use spell-check effectively. When writing, I can construct sentences correctly, avoiding run-on sentences and fragments.	I am known as an excellent speller. I can spell words most people cannot, and I catch spelling errors made by others. When writing, I can correctly use a variety of sentence structures.
Speaking/ Communication Skills	I am uncomfortable speaking to others, but I am developing my ability to carry on a conversation and use a friendly tone. I can answer questions when I am asked, but I sometimes have difficulty keeping the conversation going, unless it is about something I am interested in.	I can usually carry on a conversation with others in person or by phone using a friendly tone. When others ask me a question, I respond appropriately and try to say something that keeps the conversation going. I can stay on topic, even if the topic is not my area of interest.	I can talk to others in person or by phone using a friendly tone. When in person, I use appropriate facial expressions and body language. I can share information, answer questions, and keep a conversation going about topics of interest to others. I try to "read" the facial expressions and body language of others.
Word Processing Skills	I can create a document, type a message (though not quickly), and save it.	I can create, type, and save documents, as well as use editing features.	I can create, type, and save documents, with speed and accuracy. I can use editing features and add graphics to documents.

Skills	Beginner	Proficient	Advanced
Microsoft Office Skills (Specify: Word, PowerPoint, Excel)	I can perform basic functions using _____.	I can perform basic functions using _____, and I can usually look up and figure out things I don't know how to do.	I know how to use _____ in ways others usually don't. Others often ask me for help!
Child Care	Under supervision, I know how to occupy children of various ages with age-appropriate toys and games.	I know how to keep children safe when an adult is not present, and I can occupy children of various ages with age-appropriate toys and games.	I have had first aid training, and I can take the appropriate actions when a child is hurt or in danger. I know how to keep children in my care safe. I understand what children are capable of at different levels of development and I know what toys and games are most appropriate for them.

Think of "abilities" as "soft skills," such as being "reliable" or "able to perform routine tasks without supervision." The following are some soft skills that many employers look for in potential employees and that tend to be strengths for many on the spectrum.

- Attention to detail
- Punctuality
- Memory / recall
- Dependability
- Consistency (ability to learn a process and carry it out with consistency)
- Ability to follow procedures
- Reliability
- Industriousness
- Ability to perform routine tasks without supervision

ACTIVITY 3.10: SKILLS AND ABILITIES

Use the Activity 3.10: Skills and Abilities worksheet to identify the skills and abilities that can be valuable to a potential employer.

ACTIVITY 3.10. Skills and Abilities

Purpose: To identify soft and hard skills and abilities that would be of interest to a potential employer; to discern a proficiency level for hard skills.

Directions:
1. *Part 1:* For each skill in the chart, read the proficiency levels. Which describes you best? Circle the level that describes your proficiency level. If none of them apply, then leave that row blank.
2. *Part 2:* Read the list of soft skills in the chart. If you think you have the skill, think of some evidence that would support an example from your own life or a comment someone else has made to you about having that skill. List your evidence on the chart. Circle the skills you think best describe you.
3. Add this to your Job Notebook.

Part 1: Skill Proficiency Levels

Skills	Beginner	Proficient	Advanced
Basic Math Skills	I am good at counting, categorizing, adding, and subtracting.	I am good at counting, categorizing, adding, subtracting, multiplying, and dividing. I can use math tools, such as a calculator, effectively. I can catch and correct my own mistakes.	I am good at adding, subtracting, multiplying, and dividing. I can calculate percentages and fractions. I use math tools, such as a calculator, effectively. I rarely make mistakes in math.
Spelling and Grammar	I spell most words correctly, and I can use spell-check effectively. When writing, I correctly use simple sentence structures.	I rarely misspell words, and I can use spell-check effectively. When writing, I can construct sentences correctly, avoiding run-on sentences and fragments.	I am known as an excellent speller. I can spell words most people cannot, and I catch spelling errors made by others. When writing, I can correctly use a variety of sentence structures.

Skills	Beginner	Proficient	Advanced
Speaking/ Communication Skills	I am uncomfortable speaking to others, but I am developing my ability to carry on a conversation and use a friendly tone. I can answer questions when I am asked, but I sometimes have difficulty keeping the conversation going, unless it is about something I am interested in.	I can usually carry on a conversation with others in person or by phone using a friendly tone. When others ask me a question, I respond appropriately and try to say something that keeps the conversation going. I can stay on topic, even if the topic is not my area of interest.	I can talk to others in person or by phone using a friendly tone. When in person, I use appropriate facial expressions and body language. I can share information, answer questions, and keep a conversation going about topics of interest to others. I try to "read" the facial expressions and body language of others.
Word Processing Skills	I can create a document, type a message (though not quickly), and save it.	I can create, type, and save documents, as well as use editing features.	I can create, type, and save documents, with speed and accuracy. I can use editing features and add graphics to documents.
Microsoft Office Skills (Specify: Word, PowerPoint, Excel)	I can perform basic functions using _____.	I can perform basic functions using _____, and I can usually look up and figure out things I don't know how to do.	I know how to use _____ in ways others usually don't. Others often ask me for help!
Child Care	Under supervision, I know how to occupy children of various ages with age-appropriate toys and games.	I know how to keep children safe when an adult is not present, and I can occupy children of various ages with age-appropriate toys and games.	I have had first aid training, and I can take the appropriate actions when a child is hurt or in danger. I know how to keep children in my care safe. I understand what children are capable of at different levels of development and I know what toys and games are most appropriate for them.

Other skills I have that are not listed in the chart:

My proficiency level is: _____ Basic; _____ Proficient; _____ Advanced
When I use this skill, I can:

Part 2

Soft Skills	I think I have this skill (Yes or No)	Evidence of this skill in my own life
Attention to detail		
Punctuality		
Memory/recall		
Dependability		
Consistency (ability to learn a process and carry it out with consistency)		
Ability to follow procedures		
Reliability		
Industriousness		
Ability to perform routine tasks without supervision		

Another soft skill I have that is not listed in this chart:

Evidence for this skill:

6. *References:* Most employers request three references. References should be people who can speak to some aspect of an applicant's suitability for a job, such as their character or skills. References might be teachers or family friends, but they should not be family members. Permission to include a person as a reference should be obtained before applying for a job. It's important to let the reference person know what job is being applied for so they are not caught by surprise if an employer contacts them.

ACTIVITY 3.11: REFERENCES

Use the Activity 3.11: References worksheet to identify three references, list their contact information, and request their permission to list the contact on the résumé.

ACTIVITY 3.11.   References

Purpose: To identify three individuals unrelated to the applicant who can speak to the applicant's character, skills and abilities, and/or fit for a particular job.

Directions:
1. Identify three people who are not related to you who know you well to include as references on your résumé. These people should be able to talk about your character, skills, and abilities, and/or your fit for the job you are applying for. You might include a teacher, a friend of your parents, a former supervisor, a person who goes to your church, or a scout leader.
2. Contact each person you wish to include as a reference. Have paper and pen handy so you can record their contact information accurately. Explain that you will soon be applying for jobs and tell them what kind of job you hope to get. Ask their permission to be included as a reference on your résumé. You might say something like this:
   Hello, Mr. Kenworth. This is Kevin Jones from Community Church. I plan to apply for a job soon as a _____, and I was wondering if I could include you as a reference. Would that be OK?
   Thank you very much.
   I'd like to be sure I have your correct contact information. (Ask the person to spell their first and last names if you are not sure of the proper spelling.)
   Would you tell me the phone number that would be best for an employer to reach you? May I have your email address, please? And a mailing address?
   Thank you.
   I'd just like to read this back to you to be sure I have everything correct.
   Thank you very much. I appreciate your willingness to be a reference for me.
3. List three people who have agreed to serve as references. Include their information on the following chart. Double-check for accuracy.
4. Include this in your Job Notebook.

First and last name of the reference	1.	2.	3.
How do you know this person? How long have you known the person?			
Place a check mark in this column when you have gotten their permission to include them as a reference.			
The mailing address of the reference: *Street address* *City* *State* *Zip code*			
The phone number of the reference, including area code			
The email address of the reference			

When revising a résumé for a particular job posting, the prospective employee needs to examine the job posting carefully to identify *required qualifications* and *preferred qualifications*. This is part of the employer's perspective on what is important! To have the best chance of getting noticed by an employer, the résumé should reference the qualifications specified by the employer. (If the applicant does not have the *required* qualifications, they should disregard the job and find another to apply for.) Some corporations utilize technologies that search for keywords in the résumé. Not referencing the required qualifications using the keywords stated in the job posting can lessen chances of getting noticed.

Since a résumé is often a "first impression," it needs to be carefully proofread. Typos and misspellings can be difficult for a writer to see, so having someone else review it is essential. Use bullet points for lists. Double-check dates and the spelling of names and cities for accuracy. Use a standard font like Times New Roman and aim to limit the résumé to one page.

The age-old dilemma of how to get a job when you have no work experience can be addressed through résumé-building activities. Job shadowing, unpaid internships, and volunteer work can help to fill out a résumé while providing valuable learning for the inexperienced job seeker.

Video Résumés

The job seeker with ASD may not only have minimal work-related experiences, but they may also have difficulty articulating their strengths and abilities verbally (an issue that will be addressed in more depth in the following chapter on job interviews). Video résumés provide a means of showcasing a job applicant's skill. A brief video can demonstrate to an employer an applicant's suitability for the position. According to Indeed.com, video résumés should focus on one element. They may be as short as 30 seconds but should be no longer than two minutes. Some video résumés will simply be a recording showing the applicant at work on a relevant task. For example, if the applicant is seeking a job busing tables at a restaurant, the video might demonstrate the applicant clearing a table and then setting up for the next guests. Video résumés may or may not include speech, but having the applicant introduce themselves and state the task they will perform is a good idea. If speaking is included, the applicant should write out a script and practice it before recording. Also, attend to grooming and hygiene, as well as appropriate attire.

ACTIVITY 3.12: RÉSUMÉ TEMPLATE

See Activity 3.12 for a Basic Résumé Template.

ACTIVITY 3.12.   Résumé Template

Full name
Mailing Address
Phone Number
Email Address

Job Objective: To obtain a position as a _____ at _____.

Relevant Experiences	Company or Employer Name and Address	Dates

Education and Training: School Name	School City and State	Dates Attended	Diploma, Certificate, or Degree Awarded

Skills	Proficiency Level

Abilities

References (Name and mailing address)	Relationship to the Applicant and Number of Years the Individual Has Known the Applicant	Phone Number with Area Code	Email Address

The applicant's portfolio can be taken on job interviews, serving as a prompt for sharing relevant strengths and experiences. See Activity 3.13.

ACTIVITY 3.13.   Portfolio

Although some of the same information could be in the Job Notebook and the Portfolio, the purpose of the Job Notebook is to be a reference for the applicant. The portfolio is for the applicant to show to the prospective employer. The portfolio should include artifacts such as photos and information that will serve as a trigger to help the applicant speak about their relevant experiences, education, skills, and abilities during an interview.

JOB APPLICATIONS

Once a basic résumé has been composed, it can be used as a reference when completing a job application. Some employers require a job application in place of or in addition to a résumé. A job application is a short form with a standard set of questions that helps to ensure that the employer evaluates all candidates on an equal basis. In addition, a standard format allows an employer to locate essential information about an applicant quickly and easily.

Most applications are accessed online. Some can be printed out, completed, and either uploaded or submitted in person. Other applications are online forms that are completed and submitted electronically. The applicant should keep their résumé nearby as they complete an application so they can refer to it for names and dates and check for accuracy.

A job application may seem easier to complete because the applicant simply responds to the employer's questions, rather than composing a document from scratch. However, this can also make things more challenging for the applicant because completing the application appropriately depends on reading ability—specifically, vocabulary knowledge, which is often an area of weakness for individuals with ASD.

The vocabulary of job applications often presents challenges. Individuals with ASD may have an extensive vocabulary related to areas of intense interest but have limited understanding of words outside of their immediate experience. In addition, they tend to focus on parts and can miss the big picture. Terms that are unfamiliar or common words used in unusual ways may also cause confusion. Job applications can be demystified by introducing applicants to the major sections commonly found on applications. This will help them to see the big picture and begin to understand the types of information an employer needs. In addition, job seekers should learn to categorize common terms, identifying synonymous terms that may appear on applications. See Table 3.3 for an explanation of common job application terms and the section of the application where they typically appear.

TABLE 3.3. Job Application Terms

Section of the Application	Terms and Abbreviations	Why the Employer Needs to Know
Personal Information	Name: First, Last, Surname, Maiden Name, Initial, Suffix (e.g., Jr., Sr., III)	Contact information; may encounter records with a maiden name
Personal Information	Mailing address: Street, Apt., Postal Code, Zip Code, Borough, Town, City, State	Contact information
Personal Information	Email address; Cell Phone, Mobile Phone, Home Phone, Office/Work Phone	Contact information
Personal Information	Emergency Contact	To know who to contact in case of emergency
Work Experience	Company, Employer, Position Held, Supervisor, Dates of Employment, Reason for Leaving	To evaluate previous work experience: how long an employee stays at a job and the kinds of work done
Education	Schools, University/College, Diploma, Degree, GPA, Graduation Date	To determine the level of education achieved by the applicant
References	Name, Designation, Relationship, Contact Information	To be able to contact references who can speak to an applicant's character or skill
Position Being Applied For	Title of Position, Salary Expected (per hour; weekly; annual salary); Negotiable; Availability; Start Date	To determine the applicant's availability for work and their expectations for pay
Demographic Information (usually optional)	Gender; marital status; age; military history; ethnicity; race	To help ensure that all applicants are sought out and evaluated fairly

Activity 3.14: Job Application Word Sort

See Activity 3.14 for vocabulary terms to sort into categories. Though many individuals with ASD have little difficulty with word recognition, comprehension is usually more challenging. Unfamiliar terms and familiar words that are used in unfamiliar ways can complicate comprehension for individuals with ASD. Word sorts help to build word concepts by making connections between words more explicit.

ACTIVITY 3.14. Job Application Word Sort

Purpose: To learn the vocabulary associated with job applications and résumés by making connections between terms.

Directions:
1. Cut apart the word cards.
2. Sort the word cards into categories. There are many ways to categorize the words. You might look for:
   a. Words found in particular sections of an application (e.g., words found in the "Contact Information" section of an application.)
   b. Synonyms (i.e., words that mean the same thing)
   c. "Words I don't understand"
3. Use a dictionary or glossary to check yourself, if necessary.
4. Explain your categories to a friend or teacher.

Personal Information	Contact Information	First Name
Last Name	Surname	Maiden Name
Initial	Suffix	Mailing Address
Street	Apt./Apartment	Postal Code
Zip Code	City	Town
Borough	State	Email Address
Cell Phone	Mobile Phone	Home Phone
Office/Work Phone	Emergency Contact	Work Experience
Employer	Company	Position
Supervisor	Boss	Reason for Leaving
Reason for Termination	Role	School
College	University	Training
Postsecondary	Diploma	Degree

Credential	GPA/Grade Point Average	Graduation Date
Title of Position	Salary	Negotiable
Emergency Contact	Reference	Annual Salary
Hourly Wage	Availability	Start Date
Demographic Information	Gender	Marital Status
Military History	Race	Ethnicity

Activity 3.15: Application Checklist

See Activity 3.15 for a checklist to evaluate job applications.

ACTIVITY 3.15.   Application Checklist

Purpose: To check the job application for accuracy and completeness.

Directions: Use the following checklist to evaluate your completed application.

Checklist

_____ Have I completed all sections of the application? If not, have I marked the blank areas with "N/A" for "not applicable"?

_____ Have I used my resources to define any unfamiliar words and understand parts of the application I am unsure of?

_____ Have I checked my application for spelling errors?

_____ Have I included the street, city, state, and zip code for all mailing addresses?

_____ Have I double-checked phone numbers for accuracy?

_____ Have I double-checked email addresses for accuracy?

_____ Have all of my references been alerted to my job search? Has each person given permission to be included as a reference?

_____ For paper applications: Is the application completed neatly, with black or blue ink? Do I know how the application is supposed to be submitted?

_____ For online applications: Have I prepared the application for submission according to the instructions (e.g., email with or without attachments; website submission)?

_____ Have I noted any deadlines for the application?

_____ Have I asked a trusted adult to read over my application?

Activity 3.16: Job Search Glossary

See Activity 3.16 for a job search glossary to add to the Job Notebook. Show students how to use the glossary as a reference when completing job applications.

ACTIVITY 3.16.   Job Search Glossary

Directions: Use the glossary as a reference when completing job applications. Add words to the glossary, as needed.

Apartment or apt.: A number given to the unit in an apartment complex where a person lives; part of the mailing address.

Annual salary: The amount of money a person earns in a year.

Availability: When a person is available to work; could be a date to start employment or the usual days and times a person is available to work.

Borough: A town or community.

Boss: A supervisor or company owner who is in charge of overseeing employees' work.

Cell phone: The number of a person's mobile phone.

City: The town or city where a person lives or where a company is located; part of the mailing address.

College: An institution of higher education that a person may attend after high school.

Company: The name of a business or corporation.

Contact information: Information an employer would need to contact the applicant, such as mailing address, phone number, and email address.

Credential: A document that provides evidence of the successful completion of a course of study.

Degree: A credential awarded upon successful completion of a course of study at a college or university.

Demographic information: Information about a person that is used for classification purposes; may include gender, race, ethnicity, age, number of years of education, etc.

Diploma: A credential awarded upon successful completion of a course of study, such as high school.

Email address: The address where a person receives electronic mail (email). Example: jsuxh@gmail.com.

Emergency contact: The name and information needed to contact the person best able to help in case of emergency; usually the name and phone number of a close relative.

Employer: The name of a person or company for which a person works.

Ethnicity: The culture of people from a particular region.

First name: The name given by parents to a child at birth.

Gender: A person's identity as male, female, or other.

Grade Point Average/GPA: A person's overall grade during a course of study, based on a four-point scale.

Graduation date: The date that a program of study is completed; an "expected graduation date" is the date one expects to graduate.

Home phone: May refer to a "landline" phone in a person's house, but could also refer to the best phone number to reach a person.

Hourly wage: The amount of money a person earns for an hour of work.

Initial: A letter followed by a period that stands for a person's name; often used in place of a middle name.

Last name: A person's family name.

M.I.: An abbreviation for "middle initial"; the first letter of a person's middle name, followed by a period.

Maiden name: A person's last name before marriage (if the spouse's name was taken).

Mailing address: The place where a person gets their mail; usually includes a street number and name, city or town, state, and zip code. Some mailing addresses use a post office box number or a rural delivery route number and box number.

Marital status: Whether a person is married, single, or divorced; should not be disclosed on a job application or during an interview.

Military history: A person's record of service for the U.S. military, such as the army or navy.

Mobile phone: The cell phone number where a person can be reached.

Negotiable: Not set; a salary that is negotiable is one to be agreed upon by the employee and employer.

Office phone: The phone number where a person can be reached when at their place of work.

Optional: A question or section of the application that you complete only if you choose to do so. You may leave it blank.

Personal information: Information an employer would need to contact the applicant, such as mailing address, phone number, and email address.

Position: The name of a particular job or role, such as "cashier."

Postal Code: A zip code; usually five digits.

Postsecondary: Occurring after high school.

Prefer not to answer: An answer choice that indicates an applicant prefers not to disclose the information.

Preferred: Often used in reference to a phone number; the one you would like an employer to use when they contact you.

Race: A social designation based on a person's physical traits, such as skin color.

Reason for leaving: The reason a person leaves a job.

Reference: A person not related to a job applicant who can speak to the person's character, skills, training, and/or fit for a job.

Role: The position a person has in their workplace; a person's job.

Salary: The money an employee earns on a regular basis for their work.

School: The place where an education is received; on job applications usually refers to high school, vocational training school, or college.

Start date: The date an employee is available to begin working.

Street: Part of the address that includes the house number and street name.

Suffix: A designation sometimes added after a name to indicate position in a family, such as "Jr." (Junior), "Sr. (Senior), "I," "II," or "III." For example, "John Smith, Jr."

Supervisor: The name of a person who oversees the work of another employee.

Surname: A person's last name.

Termination: The end of employment; can be initiated by the employee or the employer.

Title: A person's position within a company.

Town: The name of the community where a person lives.

Training: Education provided by an instructor.

University: An institution of higher education that a person may attend after high school.

Wages: Money earned by an employee for work.

Work experience: A list of the companies a person has worked for in the past, including company name, address, and dates of employment.

Work phone: The phone number where a person can be reached when at their place of work.

Zip code: The five-digit number assigned to an area by the postal service.

MORE ABOUT PROFESSIONALISM

Though an applicant may have to submit many applications before receiving an invitation to interview, once an application or résumé is submitted, the applicant should anticipate being contacted. A prospective employer usually contacts an applicant by phone or email. The purpose of the contact may be to ask clarifying questions about the applicant's experiences or to schedule an interview. Every call should be answered as if it may be the potential employer (even if the applicant is very sure it's their mother calling!). Job seekers should write out scripts for talking with a prospective employer on the phone and role-play. Also, job seekers should practice responding to emails in a professional manner, as discussed earlier in this chapter.

SUMMARY

Though autism can complicate the job application process, with support, job seekers can learn to prepare a résumé and job application that showcase the many skills and strengths they have to offer an employer. By learning what an employer needs to know, the parts of a résumé and job application, and commonly used vocabulary, the mystery of the job application process is minimized.

CHAPTER 4

The Job Interview

Jen enters the Rite Aid, clenching and unclenching her fists. She walks up to the cashier who is working with a customer and loudly states, "I need to see the manager!" Both the cashier and customer are startled and surprised, as she appears to be angry. She continues to clench and unclench her fists, not looking at the cashier. As the cashier finishes with the customer, Jen states again, "I need to see the manager at 2:00 p.m. and it's 2:05 p.m." The cashier goes to the back of the store and says to the manager, "There is a weird, angry girl here to see you. She must be your 2:00 p.m. interview." Unknowingly, Jen has already made a poor first impression.

THINGS TO THINK ABOUT

- What implicit and explicit biases are built into current hiring processes?
- To what extent is neurodiversity included in diversity equity and inclusion (DEI) awareness and training?
- What kinds of judgments are employers likely to make about an applicant during the job interview? What do they base these judgments on? How does this impact the applicant with ASD?
- What kinds of challenges is the individual with ASD likely to struggle with during the interview process?

BEFORE THE INTERVIEW

To Disclose or Not to Disclose

As individuals on the autism spectrum begin the job search, they must decide whether they will disclose their disability, and, if so, at what point in the process they will disclose. The Americans with Disabilities Act (ADA) does not require disclosure of the disability until an accommodation is needed. Individuals must decide if it's in their best interest to disclose; however, communication and social challenges with coworkers and supervisors tend to be a primary factor that hinders job performance. Some individuals with disabilities feel they should disclose as early in the process as possible, while others believe that the disability only needs to be disclosed if accommodations are necessary. There are pros and cons to both approaches (see Table 4.1). This is a personal preference, but there should be a discussion to help the individual with ASD to make an informed decision. If an individual discloses prior to the job interview, they may be able to get needed accommodations for the interview. If a disability is disclosed, possible accommodations at the time of the interview may include a phone or Zoom initial interview, interview questions provided prior to the interview, a vocational coach in attendance, or a different location if transportation is an issue.

TABLE 4.1. Possible Pros and Cons of Disclosure

Pros	Cons
• Possible accommodations during the interview process • Employer may be more understanding and willing to accommodate • Accommodations will be provided • Employer assistance in finding the correct job match based on individual's needs/preferences • Possible autism awareness training for supervisors/coworkers • Awareness of strengths/weaknesses on the job	• Stereotyping • Discrimination • Low expectations • Bullying from coworkers

See Activity 4.1 for a role play about disclosing a disability.

ACTIVITY 4.1. Role-Play a Disclosure Discussion

Help the student with the language he/she might use to identify their disability. This is a personal decision and one that students must be taught in order to advocate for themselves. In the role-play, the student should also provide characteristics/preferences that are unique to him/her and explain how those characteristics impact job performance. Perhaps provide two strengths and two challenges. Additionally, help the individual identify possible accommodations or supports that might be helpful in doing the job. See the following example between an individual with ASD and an interviewer:

Interviewer: Hello. Please tell me a little about yourself.
IASD: I am autistic and want to let you know a little about that and how it helps me do my job.
Interviewer: Okay. Please tell me.
IASD: I like a schedule. It is helpful if I have the same schedule each week. This is helpful for the job, because I will be dependable.
IASD: I don't like big crowds. If I am working in an office with one or two people, I am better able to focus on my work.
IASD: I will ask a lot of detailed questions when learning a new job but once I learn it, I will do it exactly as I am taught.

Understanding How Conversation Works

Despite having average or above average intellectual ability, characteristics of ASD can impair an individual's expected performance at an interview. Difficulty with verbal communication may include

- difficulty engaging in conversation, including how to start a conversation and how to keep it going;
- difficulty with reciprocity (i.e., the back and forth of conversation: I ask a question; you respond; I ask a follow-up question; you respond);
- poor reporting of events, including inability to articulate an experience or skill; and
- shorter utterances, such as "yes/no" answers or nodding the head. (Morgan et al., 2014)

Difficulty with nonverbal communication may include

- difficulty with eye contact: staring too long or not making eye contact at all; and
- facial affect: may be flat and unexpressive or unable to hide responses that are felt (i.e., disgust when told that the job entails cleaning the bathrooms).

ACTIVITY 4.2. Keeping the Conversation Going

To help individuals understand how to engage in conversation, illustrate with a game of "catch." Explain that a conversation is like tossing the ball back and forth. One person says something (toss the ball to a partner) and the other responds (partner catches the ball). If the person responds with a one-word answer, such as "Yes," the conversation (or the game of "catch" ends). It is that person's responsibility to keep the conversation going by responding in a way that engages the other person, such as by adding explanation or asking a question (toss the ball back).

Help the person understand that an interview is a special kind of conversation. Unlike a conversation with a friend or family member where our goal is to keep the conversation going, an interview is more like a game of catch a teenager might have with a younger niece or nephew. The teenager takes charge of the game, tossing the ball and hoping the child will catch the ball with both hands. The child's task is not to drop the ball. Similarly, the interviewer takes charge of the conversation. They ask the questions, hoping the interviewee will give a clear answer to the question. The interviewee's task is to respond with a thorough and thoughtful response—a "two-hands" kind of an answer!

Preparation to Reduce Anxiety

Since individuals with ASD suffer from higher rates of anxiety than their neuro-typical peers, planning ahead will help reduce the inevitable stress and anxiety an individual will feel during the interview process. Ways to avoid undue stress include the following.

1. Be sure the individual knows where to report and what time. Perhaps have them practice a "dry run" the week prior to the interview.
2. Discuss what type of stereotypic behaviors are appropriate ways to control stress and nervousness the day of the interview (i.e., instead of fist clenching, use a stress ball).
3. Be sure the individual understands the job expectations and skills needed, and that these are a match for their abilities and preferences.
4. Prepare the individual with the types of questions that will be asked during the interview and appropriate answers.

5. Role-play to allow the individual to practice.

As mentioned in Chapter 2, job matching will be very important. Be sure that the individual has a clear understanding of the job requirements and skills and that these are accurate matches for their strengths, skills, and preferences. Interviewers will always ask the interviewee to discuss their skills and abilities as they relate to the job. The video *How to Communicate Your Strengths in a Job Interview* might be helpful: https://youtu.be/PapEY2EcoMI. They will also often ask about an individual's weaknesses. Individuals with ASD are very literal and often do not fully comprehend the subtleties of tact, metaphors, or figurative language. It is best to be honest and blunt about the individual's weaknesses and challenges. Provide direction on how to talk about these strengths and weaknesses in a job interview. Often individuals with ASD need to be given the vocabulary to articulate their strengths and weaknesses, so practice activities are helpful.

Other ways to help reduce anxiety in preparation for the interview include the following.

- Talking with a close mentor to understand the job description and responsibilities so that the individual will be able to speak to his/her skills, experiences, and knowledge as it applies to the job.
- Honestly articulating strengths and weaknesses.
- Reviewing possible interview questions online.
- Writing out note cards.
- Practicing mock interviews.
- Doing a "practice run" by going to the job site and observing the job in action and the environment to better understand the requirements.
- Using a portfolio that highlights skills, abilities, and work experiences as a prompt to articulate strengths.

The key to reducing anxiety and having a successful interview is practice, practice, practice! Provide as much preparation as possible, including exposure to the types of questions that will be asked and practicing the answers, role-plays, augmented reality interview training, and mock interviews with professionals.

MAKING A GOOD FIRST IMPRESSION

"You never get a second chance to make a first impression"—so the saying goes, and nowhere is this more important than in the job search. First impressions can be lasting, and a negative first impression can be difficult to overcome, especially in the competitive job market. Because individuals with ASD do not always have a sense of how others perceive them, they may not be aware of the impression they make upon others. Explicit instruction in various aspects of professionalism can help the applicant with ASD to make a positive impression during their first interactions with a prospective employer.

Phone Calls and Email Correspondence

Once an individual has submitted an application, they should treat every phone call as if it could be from the employer (even if they know their friend always calls at that particular time of the day). Phone calls should be answered with a pleasant tone and clear speech. Use the script in Activity 4.3 to practice role-play a phone call from an employer. Email correspondence should be professional in tone, focused, and free of abbreviations and spelling errors. All contact information should be included in the email. See Chapter 3 for samples.

ACTIVITY 4.3.   Phone Script: Call for an Interview

Purpose: To answer a call and carry on a phone conversation professionally with a prospective employer.
Phone rings ... even though the applicant is pretty sure the call is from her mother, she answers professionally, with a pleasant tone.

Applicant (Cara Rodriquez): Hello?
Employer: This is Mr. Jensen calling from Air Products Company. Is this Cara Rodriquez?
Applicant: Yes, this is Cara.
Employer: Cara, I have reviewed your application, and I would like to talk further with you about your qualifications for the job of stock clerk. Would you be willing to come for an interview?
Applicant: Yes, thank you. I'd be happy to come for an interview.
Employer: That's great to hear. We are doing interviews next week. Would you be able to come on Monday at 10:00?
Applicant: Yes, I will be there Monday at 10:00. Should I come to the main entrance of the building?
Employer: Yes, use the main entrance. The reception desk is right near the entrance. Let the receptionist know when you arrive, and they will direct you to my office.
Applicant: Thank you, Mr. Jensen. I look forward to meeting you.
Employer: I am looking forward to meeting you, as well. Goodbye.
Applicant: Good-bye.

Hygiene

Body odor, greasy hair, or dirt under the fingernails can derail an interview before it starts! The Hygiene Checklist in Activity 4.4 can help job seekers to show up on interview day neat and clean. In addition, good hygiene practices are essential to good health, and just as important to good relationships with future coworkers.

ACTIVITY 4.4. Hygiene Checklist

Purpose: To make a good first impression by being neat and clean; to maintain cleanliness and good health.

Directions:
1. Place this checklist somewhere you will see it when you get ready for the day.
2. Use the checklist to prepare before leaving your house.

Daily Hygiene Checklist

_____ I have taken a shower within the past 24 hours (or less if I have done a lot of physical work).

_____ My hair is clean and combed.

_____ My face is washed. *(Girls: You may want to apply light makeup.)*

_____ I brush my teeth after waking up and before bed (and after eating, if necessary). I used dental floss and mouthwash.

_____ My hands are washed. My fingernails are trimmed and clean.

_____ I applied deodorant or antiperspirant.

_____ My clothing has been laundered. It has no stains, wrinkles, missing buttons, or tears.

_____ I have not overused cologne or perfume.

Dress

Though many workplaces have adopted casual dress, appearing for an interview in casual attire is usually not wise. The video found at https://youtu.be/g6xufGeyaMU can help to begin a conversation about how to dress (and how not to dress) for an interview. In general, applicants should try to find out how employees of the company dress and aim to dress slightly more formally. Since individuals with ASD may have difficulty discerning appropriate attire, be explicit about the types of clothing that should and should not be worn. Avoid jeans and T-shirts with printed messages or pictures. For men, collared shirts, such as polo shirts or button-down shirts and khakis or dress pants are usually appropriate. For women, khakis, dress pants, dresses, or skirts are usually acceptable. Dresses or skirts should be of a modest length. Clothing should be clean and free of stains, wrinkles, tears, or missing buttons. Shoes should be clean and appropriate for the outfit without showing obvious signs of wear. Any jewelry or makeup should enhance rather than detract from the applicant's overall appearance.

Activity 4.5 helps students learn to dress appropriately for the workplace.

ACTIVITY 4.5. Dress for Success

Part of dressing appropriately for an interview is knowing the culture of the workplace. The goal is to dress just a little bit more formally than the workplace culture. Research a particular jobsite. What do the employees wear? If you were going to interview for a job there, what would you wear? Find pictures or photos of clothing, hair styles, jewelry, and shoes. Create a collage to show how you would dress for the interview.

Handshakes and Personal Space

Individuals with ASD may have sensory issues that cause them to avoid personal contact. Though concerns about the COVID-19 virus and other communicable diseases have resulted in changes in expectations for personal contact, if an employer extends their hand, it is considered polite to respond with a firm (but not too firm) handshake. However, the applicant should not initiate a handshake; not everyone is comfortable with that level of contact. Those with sensory issues may prefer to have a greater sense of personal space. Some on the spectrum may not respect others' needs for personal space because they don't understand it. A sense of "personal space" varies by culture, but according to Indeed (2022), three feet is generally considered acceptable during an interview. Help students to estimate and adopt an appropriate distance from others as they communicate.

Eye Contact

Eye contact communicates essential information to an interview, such as professionalism, interest, confidence, and politeness. However, maintaining appropriate eye contact is especially difficult for individuals with ASD. Some may avoid eye contact, and others may stare. Avoiding eye contact can suggest a lack of confidence and a lack of interest, whereas, eye contact that is too prolonged can suggest aggression or intimidation. Difficulty with eye contact is one reason an applicant may want to disclose their disability.

Small Talk

Individuals on the spectrum tend to take information literally, so small talk is often misinterpreted. An interviewer may begin the interview by making conversation with the applicant. Such "small talk" is not only a way of putting nervous applicants at ease, but also of gaining an initial sense of the applicant's personality. Questions and comments about the weather, the traffic, or time spent waiting for the interview to begin are common attempts to make conversation with the applicant. Those with ASD may interpret questions literally and respond bluntly in ways that make them appear rude or negative in their outlook. For example, responding to a question about the traffic with, "Yeah, it took me a half hour to get here and this driver cut me off so I flipped him the bird" will likely suggest to the interviewer that an applicant is a complainer who would not have much patience with coworkers or customers.

INTERVIEW ETIQUETTE

As mentioned previously in this chapter, applicants may want to make a "dry run" to the interview site. If the location is unfamiliar, making the trip ahead of time to check out the route, parking, and entrances can eliminate some anxiety and help to prevent a late arrival. The interview essentially begins from the moment an applicant sets foot on the property. It's possible that the person encountered in the parking lot is the interviewer or a prospective coworker, so everyone needs to be treated with courtesy and politeness! The applicant should show up a few minutes prior to the scheduled interview time and build in time for a trip to the restroom. The applicant should politely let a staff member know they have arrived for the interview, and then follow instructions for the place to wait. The applicant should wait as patiently as possible without excessive fidgeting and movement or excessive questioning of people around them.

Additional tips for nonverbal communication during an interview can be found at https://www.indeed.com/career-advice/interviewing/how-to-sit-in-an-interview.

Listening Skills Training

Listening well is an essential but sometimes overlooked part of successful interviewing. Anxiety can cause an applicant to focus on how they will respond, rather than what the interviewer is actually saying. Difficulties with turn-taking in conversation can lead to inappropriate interruptions. Jumping to conclusions or prejudging a speaker's intent can result in misinterpretation of an interviewer's question. A four-step reminder (adapted from Center on Transition Innovations, 2020) can help the interviewee prepare to listen well:

Focus on the speaker's message.
Avoid interrupting.
Keep an open mind—don't prejudge.
Eye contact communicates your interest!

Understanding the Why Behind the Questions

Theory of Mind deficits, that is, difficulty reasoning about other peoples' mindsets (Ashkam, 2022), and a tendency to take information literally can complicate the job seeker's ability to understand the motivations of an employer in asking particular questions. This can result in the interviewee giving too much or too little information or inappropriately responding to the question. For example, when an interviewer begins the interview with "Were you waiting long?" the purpose of the question is not to ascertain how many minutes the applicant sat in the waiting room, but rather to put the interviewee at ease by engaging in small talk. Similarly, many interview questions asked by an employer are designed to give the interviewer access to information about the applicant that is not found on a résumé—the so-called soft skills that are sometimes just as valued by an employer as the hard skills. It is helpful to explain these types of questions and practice them in role-play to provide feedback on appropriate answers and language use. Table 4.2 lists some common interview questions and the rationale behind the question.

TABLE 4.2. The Whys of Interview Questions

Common Interview Questions	Rationale for the Question
Tell me about yourself.	How well do you speak? Are you professional? Do you have an evidently positive or negative attitude? Do you focus on yourself or the job? What is your personality like? *(Keep in mind that the interviewer has already read the applicant's resume!)*
How did you hear about the position?	What strategies did you use to find the job? What appealed to you about the job? Did a current employee recommend you? If so, who?
What type of work environment do you prefer?	Will you be a good fit?
Tell about a time you experienced stress or pressure and how you typically respond to stressful situations.	Can you handle pressure in the workplace?
If you are assigned a group project, what role do you prefer to take? How do you feel about group work?	Can you work well with others? Do you prefer working alone? Are you a take-charge person or do you prefer to work in the background?
If you were asked to work a day that you were not assigned, would you be willing to come in?	Are you flexible? Will this job be a priority to you?
Our company policy is that illicit drug use of any kind is not tolerated. Would you be willing to do regular drug screenings?	Are you willing to participate in the screenings (as other employees do on a regular basis)? *The question is not asking if you use illegal drugs, but if you are willing to be tested as a means of proving you are not taking drugs.*
What are your strengths?	Can you speak confidently and appropriately about your strengths? Are the things you consider strengths valued in this workplace culture? Do you have achievements that would prove valuable in this setting?
What are your weaknesses?	In what areas do you feel that you need to grow? Are your areas of growth directly related to success in the job being applied for?
Why do you want to work here?	Do your skills match the job? How badly do you want to work here? How committed are you likely to be to the job? Have you researched the company? Do you know what the job culture is like, and will you fit in?

(continued)

TABLE 4.2. *(continued)*

Common Interview Questions	Rationale for the Question
Where do you see yourself five years from now?	Is this job likely to be a long-term commitment for you or a stepping-stone to something else? Do you want to grow in your knowledge of this field?
Why should we hire you?	Are you the best person for the job? Do you have skills and abilities that will benefit the company? Do you care about the employer's needs or just your own need for a paycheck?
What is your ideal company?	Are you a good match for this company and the work culture? Do your values align with those of the company?
Do you have any questions for me?	Are you focused on your own needs and how the job will benefit you? Have you taken time to learn about the company?

Note. Adapted from Oliver (2021) and Peterson (2023).

Augmented Reality and Other Technology Tools to Practice Interview Skills

Augmented reality (AR) has been used successfully to train for a variety of fields. There are several benefits to using AR with individuals with disabilities. Augmented reality allows individuals to interact in real-world social contexts that are controllable and malleable, lessening perceived risks. Burke and colleagues (2018) showed that the use of AR tools do, in fact, help to minimize anxiety when used instructionally for those with disabilities, particularly those with ASD. AR allows for repeated trials with accurate real-life situations that provide the learner with opportunities to detect and correct errors without adverse effects; limit sensory input to visual and auditory, thereby minimizing distractions; pause or stop the simulation to receive coaching (many AR platforms have feedback built in); and provide a record of performance that demonstrates progress.

Augmented reality has been shown to improve communication for individuals with ASD and other disabilities. The ability to articulate strengths effectively and respond appropriately to a variety of questions can be improved through AR and other video-based interventions (VBIs) (Burke, et al., 2018; Hayes et al., 2015; Munandar et al., 2020), though Reichow and Volkmar (2009) caution that video modeling in and of itself may be insufficient to promote behavioral changes. Notably, AR has been used effectively to improve the ability of individuals with ASD to read nonverbal cues, specifically facial expressions (Chen et al., 2015), as well as to understand alternative points of view (Kumazaki et al., 2019).

APPLICATION OF AR TO INTERVIEWING SKILLS TRAINING

The poor employment outcomes cited in the introduction can be attributed, at least in part, to the fact that most jobs require skills that are core deficits for individuals with ASD. For example, individuals with ASD have difficulty with social functioning, such as initiating interactions with others, engaging in the reciprocity of communication, and understanding pragmatic language including body language, voice tone, and the use of figurative language. Interviews require individuals to be effective in verbal and nonverbal communication; proficient in conveying the knowledge and skills they possess to do the job; and effective social and interpersonal skills to work with supervisors, coworkers, and customers (Arter et al., 2021). Explicit job interviewing skills training practice is necessary to improve employment outcomes for individuals with ASD. Using AR can help in training for job interview skills by reducing barriers, allowing multiple practice attempts, and providing individuals feedback to improve performance.

One software platform that has been shown to be promising is SIMmersion augmented reality job interview training system (AR-JITS; Arter et al., 2021; Smith et al., 2015). The AR-JITS by Immersive Simulations (https://www.simmersion.com/) provides interactive role-play scenarios with realistic avatars for a variety of situations, including coaching for improved performance, cognitive behavioral therapy, suicide prevention training, and interview training. The programs have multiple features that support individuals with ASD. One simulation is "Job Interview Training Featuring Molly Porter." This specific platform uses a simulated human resources interviewer named "Molly Porter." There is a programmed question bank with over 1,000 items on a wide range of topics designed to improve success in a professional interview. The program has built-in, universally designed support, such as text-to-speech and speech-to-text for those with low reading and typing abilities; a menu of possible responses to assist the respondent; a virtual coach that provides visual (thumbs up, thumbs in the middle, or thumbs down) and written, in-the-moment feedback; and several levels of challenge: easy, medium, and difficult. Molly Porter's responses, facial expressions, and body language change based on the respondent's answers and level of difficulty. A written transcript of the questions and answers is also provided with an explanation about why their answer was best or why another would have been better to use as further feedback and teaching opportunities. A short video clip of job interviewing training with Molly can be viewed at https://youtu.be/YJZIZzbq6rM.

Below is a screenshot of the AR-JITS. On the left is "Molly." She asks the question verbally and the text of the question appears below her. In the lower right-hand corner of Molly's screen is the virtual coach who will offer visual real-time feedback (thumbs up, thumbs sideways, thumbs down) and a text explanation of her feedback. On the right side of the screen is the answer bank. Students can choose from multiple responses, some appropriate and some not. These answers can be read independently or read aloud by the text reader.

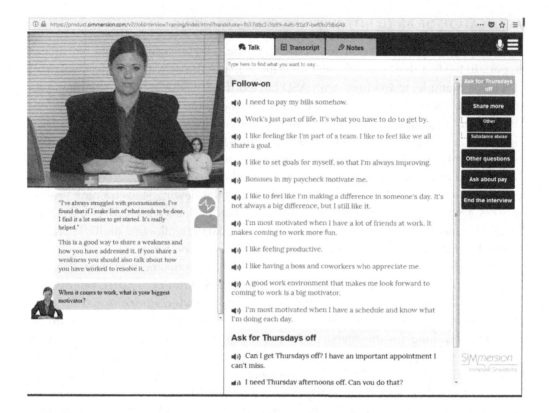

JOB INTERVIEW TRAINING FEATURING MOLLY PORTER

Arter and colleagues (2021) used AR-JITS with a small number of high school students with a primary diagnosis of autism spectrum disorder. Students were required to complete a minimum of three trials achieving 80% or better before moving on to the next difficulty level. Overall, students demonstrated a trend toward improvement in the areas of professionalism, including turn-taking, time engaged in conversation during the interview, and appropriate answers. The areas of turn-taking and increased minutes in conversation were particularly promising given that many individuals with ASD often lack communication skills in the area of reciprocity. After each session, the transcript was reviewed, and strengths and weaknesses were discussed with each student. With support, students were able to improve their scores over time. More recently, SIMmersion has developed job interview training for transition youth.

The following is a screenshot of the transcript. It shows the question asked by Molly, the student response, and a written explanation of why the answer was correct or if there was a better answer. Instructors can use these transcripts to review with individual students the correct and incorrect answers. The transcripts can also be reviewed with individual students, or whole-class instruction can be provided based on common mistakes.

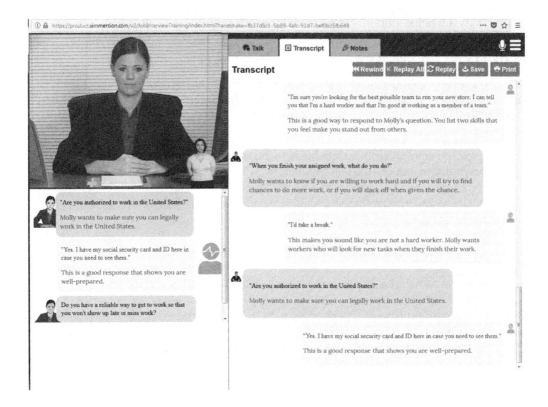

Other Technology Tools to Support Interviewing Skills

One way to create equity, inclusion, and access is through the use of technology and extended realities, specifically virtual and augmented reality. However, not all institutions have access to extended realities platforms like SIMmersion. Other tools can be utilized to develop interviewing skills, albeit with more preparation on the part of the teacher. Table 4.3 provides some alternative tools.

TABLE 4.3. Technology Tools to Support Interviewing Skills

Technology Tool	Description
Zoom	Zoom is an online communication tool. Mock interviews can be conducted and interviews can be recorded for later analysis.
Voice Thread	Voice Thread is a web-based tool with the potential for asynchronous interaction between an interviewer and an interviewee. Interview questions can be recorded and may be audio-recorded, video-recorded, or text. The interviewee can respond to questions in any of the three modes.
EdPuzzle	EdPuzzle is a tool that allows prerecorded videos of interviews to be uploaded with embedded prompts. Students have to respond to the prompt before going on with the video.
Flipgrid	Flipgrid is an interactive tool that allows students to watch video content and generate a video response. Students can interact this way with the teacher or with peers.

Activity 4.6 helps students to prepare for mock interviews.

ACTIVITY 4.6. Mock Interviews

Role-play interviews using a platform like SIMmersion or other technology tools. The questions in Figure 4.1 may be helpful if you are not using a platform specifically designed for job interview preparation. Prior to the mock interviews, prepare students using the following steps (adapted from Arter et al., 2021):

1. *Job Exploration and Matching:* Explore the demands of various jobs and the need for a match between the demands of a job and the interests, skills, and abilities of the job seeker. (See Chapter 2.)
2. *Résumé Development and Job Applications:* Completing a résumé and job applications will help the prospective employee better articulate their qualifications for a particular job. (See Chapter 3.)
3. *Professional Introductions:* Help the prospective employee understand the importance of making a good first impression. Provide positive and negative examples and role-play the following: eye contact, handshakes, and the "small talk" typically used at the start of an interview. (See this chapter.)
4. *Interview Preparation:* Discuss professionalism, including the need to respond professionally to any calls or emails from a potential employer and interview etiquette. (See this chapter.) Have students work in pairs to develop an appropriate response to the interview question posed by the teacher. Discuss the interviewer's reason for asking the question (see Figure 4.2 in this chapter) and the pros and cons of possible responses. Next, have students work in pairs, with one playing the part of the interviewer and the other being the job applicant. Discuss responses and the match between the response and the interviewer's reason for asking the question.
5. *Mock Interviews:* Engage in mock interviews using a platform such as SIMmersion or using technology tools such as those discussed in Figure 4.2. Provide feedback to students and allow the opportunity to improve their responses.

People on the autism spectrum often struggle with job interviews, yet they have much to offer in the workplace. This video by CBC News—People with Autism Recruited for Skilled Jobs—shows how a company recruits people with Autism for firms that need skilled workers. The video illustrates that despite not interviewing well, individuals with ASD can be successful if given the right opportunity and appropriate accommodations.

ADDITIONAL RESOURCES

- 10 Things to Know About Autism and Employment: https://www.verywellhealth.com/things-you-need-to-know-about-autism-and-employment-4159850#citation-7
- Autism Statistics and Facts: https://www.autismspeaks.org/autism-statistics-asd
- Top ten employers: https://www.verywellhealth.com/top-autism-friendly-employers-4159784
- Speech and communication: https://www.verywellhealth.com/speech-vs-communication-260566
- Dressing for an interview: https://www.youtube.com/watch?v=g6xufGeyaMU
- Handshakes: https://youtu.be/ZV_VpXVMVqw

CHAPTER 5

The Hidden Curriculum of the Job Place

....

Soft Skills on the Job

Employee: (On the computer while a customer waits).
Supervisor: Are you looking up the order for that customer?
Employee: No, I have to answer my email first.
Supervisor: The employee handbook indicates you are not supposed to be checking personal email during work hours.
Employee: No, it says no personal phone calls. I'm not making a call.

THINGS TO THINK ABOUT

- In this scenario, does the employee intend to violate company policy and alienate the customer and supervisor?
- What hidden curriculum does the employee with ASD miss?
- If there are repeated incidents similar to this scenario, what is the outcome for employment?
- How do we support and teach individuals with ASD to understand and interpret the hidden curriculum and respond appropriately?

Most of us know that an employee handbook cannot cover all possible scenarios of what to do and not do at work. Employers assume that employees will "read between the lines" and use common sense as to the meaning of the workplace rules and how they apply to a variety of different situations. In this scenario, most neurotypical individuals would understand not to make a customer wait while you engage in personal tasks, as well as not to argue with your supervisor when you are corrected. However, individuals with ASD and other disabilities are often concrete and literal. They have difficulty interpreting social situations, body language, and tone. Due to the lack of theory of mind, they are not able to put themselves in other people's shoes to understand perspectives or offer empathy. In fact, not understanding or interpreting the hidden curriculum

....

correctly may be the number one reason that individuals with ASD have difficulty finding and keeping employment. Despite the movement toward diversity, equity, and inclusion (DEI) in all workplaces, neurodiversity is not always included in this awareness and training. In fact, many of the factors we consciously or unconsciously use to determine if individuals will be competent employees are biased. Watch this TED Talks to learn why autistic unemployment rates are so high: https://youtu.be/FVZu557_k04. Until workplaces are truly inclusive, we need to support individuals with ASD in how to interact and be successful in the current system. This success is incumbent on knowing, understanding, and reacting appropriately to the hidden curriculum.

THE HIDDEN CURRICULUM: WHAT IS IT?

The hidden curriculum refers to the unscripted learning that is not formally taught. It includes the social skills that individuals learn implicitly from specific environments and individuals. Individuals with disabilities do not pick up on the hidden curriculum and often have to be taught these soft skills explicitly. This is especially true for individuals with ASD (Myles et al., 2013). The hidden curriculum is assumed knowledge that is universally understood by neurotypical individuals. It is generally not explicitly taught because it is considered known and understood by all. "Its content is typically reflected in expectations, guidelines, attitudes, values, beliefs, terminology, behavior, and other messages that are conveyed indirectly through inferences and assumptions" (Myles et al., 2013, p. 2). The hidden curriculum is the assumed and accepted behaviors and norms of an organization or culture, unwritten rules, or unspoken expectations.

The diversity of the workforce can further complicate an understanding of the hidden curriculum of the workplace. Culture, language, ability, and gender are just some of the ways coworkers may differ from one another. Acknowledging and responding to differences must be done respectfully. Members of a particular sociocultural group often share common beliefs, values, ways of communicating, and behaviors and ways of doing things. Individuals with ASD may consider coworkers from different sociocultural groups as odd or puzzling, but verbalizing those observations may be viewed as rude and intolerant. Talk to students about the value of diversity in the workplace and discuss examples of the sociocultural differences they may encounter.

> *Tip: Though respect for those of different sociocultural groups is expected, understanding all of the various norms is not. When working with a person of a sociocultural group you are not familiar with, finding out more about the group through online research or other means can facilitate a more positive working relationship. Knowledge of the group's norms can help to promote tolerance and respect, as well as provide topics for conversation.*

Activity 5.1: Role-Play: Showing Respect for Differences

After discussing the ways in which coworkers may differ from one another and the value of diversity in the workplace, look at examples of differences such as

- dress,
- language and ways of communicating,
- celebration of holidays,
- religion,
- family,
- food,
- concept of time, and
- sense of personal space.

Then role-play showing respect for differences. A sample script is included in Activity 5.1.

ACTIVITY 5.1. Role-Play: Showing Respect for Differences

Purpose: To help students respond to sociocultural differences respectfully.

Directions:

1. Brainstorm a list of ways coworkers may differ from one another.
2. Discuss how diversity among coworkers can be valuable.
3. Look at examples of potential sociocultural differences among coworkers, such as:
   - Dress
   - Language and ways of communicating
   - Celebration of holidays
   - Religion
   - Family
   - Food
   - Concept of time
   - Sense of personal space
4. Role-play ways to show respect. Sample scripts are provided:

Script 1
Setting: In the lunchroom of the workplace.

Coworker 1: (staring at coworker's lunch) What is that?
Coworker 2: It is called Mughali Chicken.
Coworker 1: It looks disgusting.
Coworker 2: (smiling) Oh no, it is really delicious. It is my family's favorite meal.
Coworker 1: (pinching nose) Pee–yoooo. It really stinks.
Coworker 2: I'm so sorry. *(Packs up her lunch and leaves the lunchroom.)*

Script 2
Setting: In the lunchroom of the workplace.

Coworker 1: I've never seen the kind of food you are eating today. Is it good?
Coworker 2: It is called Mughali Chicken. My family is from India and it is one of our favorite meals.

Coworker 1: It smells different from the food I normally eat. What kind of ingredients do you use?

Coworker 2: (smiling) In addition to the chicken, it has cashew nuts and some wonderful spices, like garlic, ginger, cinnamon, cardamom, and turmeric.

Coworker 1: I like to eat cinnamon on my toast, but I've never had it with chicken before! And I've never heard of the other spices you mentioned.

Coworker 2: Would you like me to bring some for you to try tomorrow?

Coworker 1: Thank you. That's very nice of you. I'm not sure I will like it, because I only eat certain foods. Perhaps you could bring me just a small spoonful I could try at home.

Coworker 2: I will be happy to do that. I will bring you some tomorrow!

Discussion Questions:

1. What does Coworker 1 notice about Coworker 2's lunch? (It looks and smells different from foods he/she is used to eating.)
2. How does Coworker 1 respond to the differences in Script 1? (With disgust.)
3. What are the effects of Coworker 1's response in Script 1? (Coworker leaves the lunchroom.) Why does this happen? (She may be embarrassed and feel like she is offending Coworker 1.)
4. In Script 2, how does Coworker 1 respond to the different food brought by Coworker 2? (Acknowledges the difference and asks questions to get more information about the food.)
5. Do you think Coworker 1 liked the smell of the food in Script 1? (How do you know?) Do you think Coworker 1 liked the smell of the food in Script 2? (The smell of the food would be the same in both scripts. However, it is considered rude to comment or make a face if you find something unpleasant about another person's meal.)
6. How do you think Coworker 2 acted toward Coworker 1 after the scene in Script 1? In Script 2? (Coworker 2 probably avoided Coworker 1 after the encounter in Script 1. After the encounter in Script 2, they probably acted friendly toward each other.
7. If Coworker 1 is especially sensitive to odors he or she considers unpleasant, what would be a respectful way to handle the situation? (Coworker 1 could quietly excuse themselves from the table and finish their lunch in another acceptable location.)

The hidden curriculum is communicated in both explicit (e.g., the employee handbook) and implicit (e.g., the boss's tone of voice) ways. The hidden curriculum is often considered "common sense" by employers; however, this is relative to what "makes sense" for neurotypical individuals, not diverse thinkers. The hidden curriculum goes beyond the employee handbook and impacts all areas of employment including work performance, safety, social interactions, and promotions. Individuals with ASD have difficulty reading and interpreting social situations, attending to nonverbal cues, and taking the perspective of others, all of which impact how one understands and responds to the hidden curriculum. Unfortunately, this is not something that can be learned easily unless there is explicit, contextual teaching of the unwritten rules, expectations, and values. Since individuals with ASD experience challenges with organizational and conceptual thinking skills, training in the hidden curriculum should be concrete and explicit. The hidden curriculum is a moving target with many influential variables, including environment, age, gender, culture, and social context. While the hidden curriculum is easily navigable for neurotypical, well-resourced individuals from the dominant socioculture, it is often very difficult to decipher for individuals with disabilities, especially those with ASD, because it requires understanding nuances and inferences, while individuals with ASD are very concrete and literal.

Lack of knowledge and understanding of the hidden curriculum can lead to barriers in social acceptability, increased stress and anxiety levels, and lower self-esteem and independence. Therefore, the hidden curriculum often creates a barrier to access for successful employment for individuals with disabilities. Individuals with ASD need to be explicitly taught the hidden curriculum of the workplace in general, as well as application to the specific company that hires them. Without this knowledge, individuals will unintentionally break rules and damage relationships with coworkers and supervisors, sometimes leading to termination of employment.

Sulaimani and Gut (2019) indicate that it is "unethical to ignore the heterogeneous and diverse nature of students in schools" (p. 30), yet we do not explicitly teach these soft skills, therefore leaving our individuals with ASD unprepared for the social demands beyond school, including employment. A deficit in theory of mind can explain inappropriate emotional reactions and expressions sometimes exhibited by individuals with ASD. In addition, the inability to recognize and attend to social cues impacts the behavior of the individual, as well as how others perceive and react to him/her. While it may be considered a hindrance to self-determination if we teach students how to act in situations, we can certainly assist them in being successful by using strategies that make them more aware of social constructs, courtesies, and norms of the broader community. For more on the hidden curriculum, check out the following website: https://autism classroomresources.com/the-hidden-curriculum-what-is-it/.

STRATEGIES FOR TEACHING THE HIDDEN CURRICULUM

Many words and phrases have different meanings across different environments, activities, and individuals, so it is difficult to generalize to different settings. Individuals with ASD should be provided with explicit instruction in regard to the hidden curriculum at the job they secure. It is best to daily discuss how to behave and appropriate responses for specific situations. Use "teachable moments" as they occur, correct missteps, and practice appropriate behaviors.

Since individuals with ASD tend to be uncensored, blunt, and honest, they are seen as rude in many contexts. It's important to explain how neurotypical individuals perceive their behaviors and responses and offer alternative, more appropriate, acceptable behaviors and responses.

Providing individuals with video modeling, social stories, and role-plays with examples and non-examples to practice specific employment situations will help support learning. Other evidence-based practices that are effective in developing social skills include modeling, peer-mediated instruction, scripting, and technology-aided instruction. Peer mentoring and video modeling are effective ways to provide authentic feedback on practiced social skills and situations. Students with ASD can practice the skill or role-play and peers can provide feedback on these skills. When individuals with ASD have difficulty conceptualizing verbal directions, visual supports can be designed. Video modeling or social narrations and role-plays that include nonverbal expressions can assist in helping individuals with ASD discover the intended message of the hidden curriculum. While some common examples to illustrate these strategies are included as possible activities, given the contextual nature of the hidden curriculum and the diversity of individuals with ASD, activities should be individualized to the needs of the student.

Interpreting and Reacting to Workplace Social Cues

Teach students to

- Be observant of facial expressions, body language, and voice tone and what it communicates. (There is software that demonstrates different emotions: http://www .silverliningmm.com/mindreading.htm.)
- Respect personal space and appropriate distancing during conversations.
- Use appropriate voice volume.
- Observe gender-related differences (e.g., women talk in the restroom; men do not).
- Notice when we make missteps and correct them.
- Pay attention to the audience—how we respond to coworkers, customers, and supervisors.
- Respond appropriately to criticism.
- Show interest—do not do other things when someone is talking to you.

Table 5.1 helps applicants to understand how their words may be interpreted by a supervisor.

TABLE 5.1. What Not to Say

What Not to Say to Your Supervisor	Why You Shouldn't Say It
"This job is boring."	Suggests a poor attitude about the job.
"You have it easy!"	Suggests that you think your supervisor does not work hard.
"It's not my fault, because . . ."	Don't pass blame onto others. Accept responsibility if you make a mistake.
"I don't want to work here forever."	Even if it is true that you only want the job for the immediate future, don't imply that you are thinking about moving on to another job. If the supervisor thinks you will soon leave the company, they may pass you over for promotions or further training.
"I'm so tired! I did some serious partying this weekend."	Coming to work unrested due to partying with friends suggests that you are not prioritizing your responsibility as an employee.

What Not to Say to a Coworker	Why You Shouldn't Say It
"You have nice legs."	Specific compliments on body parts are viewed as sexual and can be considered harassment.
"On Saturday I threw up the spaghetti I had for lunch all over the floor."	It's impolite to discuss health-related issues, especially in descriptive detail. People get grossed out! Also, they may be concerned that you are still contagious.
"Are you pregnant?"	Even if a coworker looks as if they are pregnant, you shouldn't assume this is the case unless they acknowledge it. They may have gained weight and it is rude to comment on people's weight or body shape.

"_____ said your new hairstyle makes you look ten years older."	Don't repeat gossip that you hear in the workplace.
"How much do you get paid an hour?"	It's rude to ask coworkers how much money they make. That's considered private unless they choose to share it with you.

What Not to Say to a Customer or Patron	Why You Shouldn't Say It
"They say the customer is always right, but you are wrong."	Your company policy may say something like, "The customer is always right." That doesn't mean that the customer is never wrong. It means that employees should never accuse a customer of being wrong. It is better to listen to their concerns, even if you don't agree with what they are saying. Then get a supervisor to help you if the customer seems upset or angry.
To the customer who has just knocked over a display or made a mess: "You should be more careful."	It may be true that a customer was not being careful, but pointing that out to the customer can be seen as rude and offensive. Most customers will be embarrassed, so it is better to reassure them that the mess can be taken care of by the employees and they should not be concerned.
"You need to calm down."	Telling an agitated customer to calm down sounds condescending and would likely result in the customer being offended, in addition to being angry and upset. It is better to acknowledge the customer's distress, tell them you are sorry they are upset, and assure them that you will do your best to help with their problem. Call a supervisor or coworker to help if you can't solve the problem yourself.
"It's good you're buying new clothes because what you're wearing looks pretty old."	Don't make negative comments about a customer's clothing or appearance. Also, be cautious in commenting about a customer's purchases or the reason they have come to your place of employment. For example, if you work in a pharmacy, commenting on the person's purchase of hemorrhoid medication could be very embarrassing.
"It's my breaktime."	If a customer has been waiting for service, they will likely get quite annoyed and feel like their business is not valued if the person they have been counting on to help them suddenly leaves with no one to take their place. Even if it is your breaktime, try to take care of all of the customers who have been waiting until a coworker comes to relieve you. If there is no one to relieve you, you may want to tell the last person in line to inform additional customers that the line is closed from that point.

Note. Many things you shouldn't say to a supervisor or coworker would also be inappropriate to say to a customer or patron. Overall, you should be cautious about commenting on a person's appearance, and do not make negative comments about your boss or your job. Adapted from Greenwald (2018).

Considerations

The following are some factors that may assist the individual with ASD to be more successful on the job. Support for learning these skills will assist in better understanding the hidden curriculum.

THINGS TO KNOW ABOUT ORGANIZATIONAL CULTURE

- How do you dress? Follow the dress code even if you don't like it.
- Personal hygiene—comb hair, brush teeth, shower, use deodorant, wear clean, appropriate clothes similar to what your coworkers are wearing to do the same job, uniform if necessary, appropriate makeup and hairstyle.
- Who do you go to with a problem?
- How much social talk is allowed? What are some topics that are appropriate to talk to your coworkers about?
- How long are breaks? Are they scheduled? Will someone tell you when to take a break?
- Who do you go to for assistance?

OTHER THINGS TO KNOW

The handbook does not include everything you need to know.

- When a supervisor asks you to do something, it is a demand, not a request.
- You do not have to like your supervisor, but you have to be pleasant and responsive. Do what they say!
- Do not correct your boss.
- Accept corrections from your boss.
- Punctuality—arrive early and prepare for shift, use bathroom and start work on time.
- "No personal calls" includes no texting.
- Work time should NOT be used for social media, personal emails, phone calls, or texting. This can be considered stealing of company time as you are being paid to do a job, not your personal business.
- No supplies should be taken for personal use. This is considered theft.
- Compliments, while considered honest, can be viewed as sexual harassment.
- Sexual harassment is against the law—unwelcome verbal, visual, and physical conduct of a sexual nature.
- Don't talk about body parts or anything related to body parts.
- Compliments should be general, not specific.
- Giving too many compliments is not genuine and can be seen as harassment.
- Do not post negative things about work or negative opinions on social media.

FACTORS THAT LEAD TO SUCCESS ON THE JOB FOR INDIVIDUALS WITH ASD

- Display a positive attitude and enthusiasm for the job.

- Ensure you have time before the day begins to organize self and tasks.
- Understand clearly the steps and responsibilities of the job.
- Know the chain of command and who is the supervisor and boss.
- Know the company policy on lateness and absences.
- Know who to notify if you are going to be late or absent and how to contact them; add their contact information into your phone.
- Know what day/time your shifts begin and end.
- Be sure you add your work shifts to your calendar or electronic device.
- Plan enough time for transportation, preparing to work, and clocking in.
- Have a plan for asking for help from coworkers or supervisor.
- Have a plan to self-regulate anxiety and stress.
- Be pleasant and make small talk with your coworkers—say hi, ask how they are, talk about the weather.

ACTIVITY 5.2: ROLE-PLAY: ATTITUDE MATTERS!

See Activity 5.2 for a role-play and discussion questions about attitude.

ACTIVITY 5.2.   Role-Play: Attitude Matters!

Purpose: To help students better understand the ways attitude is communicated in the workplaces.

Directions:
1. Select two individuals to role-play the two scenarios.
2. Read through the scripts together with appropriate intonation. (The teacher or coach may model the reading using different intonation and expression.)
3. Practice any suggested nonverbal actions.
4. Present the role-plays to the class. Ask students to identify verbal and nonverbal cues that suggest positive or negative attitudes.

Script 1:
Supervisor: Terry, I see you finished the job I gave you. How about if you help Chris with the filing?
Terry: (smiling and making eye contact with the supervisor) Sure, I'd be happy to help! Do you know what office she is working in?
Supervisor: I'm not sure of the room number, but it's the office near Human Resources.
Terry: That's no problem. I know where Human Resources is, so I'm sure I can find the correct office. *(Leaves immediately to find Chris.)*

Script 2:
Supervisor: Terry, I see you finished the job I gave you. How about if you help Chris with the filing?
Terry: (not looking at the Supervisor) No, I don't really like filing.
Supervisor: (surprised by Terry's response) Terry, I really need you to help Chris. Please go and help her with the filing.
Terry: (looking disgusted; swings arm in frustration) Well, if I have to. But I don't know where Chris is working.
Supervisor: I don't know the room number, but it's the office near Human Resources.

Terry: How am I supposed to help with filing if I don't know what room Chris is in?
Supervisor: Never mind, Terry. I will ask someone else to help.
Terry: Good, because I really hate filing.

Discussion Questions
1. What does the supervisor mean when he/she says, "How about if you help Chris . . . ?" Is the supervisor asking Terry whether he/she wants to help? What would be another way to say what the supervisor means?
2. Would an employer be more likely to value Terry as an employee in Script 1 or Script 2?
3. What verbal responses suggested a positive attitude in Script 1? What nonverbal responses?
4. What verbal responses suggested a poor attitude in Script 2? What nonverbal responses?
5. When the supervisor in Script 2 says they will ask someone else to help, is this really a good thing for Terry? Why or why not? What do you think the supervisor is thinking about Terry as an employee?

THINGS AN EMPLOYER CAN DO TO ASSIST WITH SUCCESS

- Provide a consistent schedule and job responsibilities.
- Provide a mentor or coworker who will initiate help and interactions.
- Maintain predictable social demands.
- Have a system to track work progress and provide ongoing feedback on job performance.
- Ensure predictable routines for breaks, lunch, and unstructured time.
- Initiate direct communication with opportunities to verify and clarify.
- Have a method for support from coworkers and supervisor.

ACTIVITY 5.3: THE SOCCSS STRATEGY FOR TEACHING HIDDEN CURRICULUM

The SOCCSS Strategy (Reinke, 2018) is a way to make use of teachable moments to help students better understand the hidden curriculum. It can be used before a situation occurs to prepare them or it can be used after to help them learn from missteps.

ACTIVITY 5.3. The SOCCSS Strategy for Teaching Hidden Curriculum

Purpose: Use to make the "hidden curriculum" of the workplace more explicit during "teachable moments" after a situation occurs or use the strategy to prepare students before a situation occurs.

Directions:
1. Identify the **SITUATION**. Identify the Five Ws (who, what, when, where, why).
2. List possible **OPTIONS**.
3. Consider the **CONSEQUENCES** of each option.
4. Make a **CHOICE** about the best course of action.
5. Come up with a **STRATEGY**, or a plan of action.
6. Try out the strategy in a **SIMULATION**.

Here's an example of SOCCSS:

SITUATION
- *Who:* Supervisor
- *What:* Cam is annoyed when her supervisor says, "I need you to work next Friday. I know you weren't scheduled, but we are really short-staffed." Cam had planned to go shopping with a friend.
- *Where:* In the breakroom
- *When:* As Cam gets ready to leave work
- *Why:* One of Cam's coworkers has an appointment and is not able to work her scheduled shift. Cam is asked to fill in. Cam becomes agitated because she was not on the schedule to work and was looking forward to spending time with her friend.

OPTION, CONSEQUENCES, CHOICE

OPTIONS	CONSEQUENCES	CHOICE
Cam can get angry and tell the supervisor "no" because Friday is not her day to work. Cam will tell the coworker she is on the schedule so she should be at work.	Cam will be seen as uncooperative and inflexible by the supervisor. Filling in for a coworker is a courtesy that is usually reciprocated. Telling a coworker she should be at work is overstepping. The supervisor is the one who approves or denies requests for changes in schedule. The coworker would likely find Cam's comment rude, and their working relationship could be damaged.	
Cam can agree to work the shift and ask her friend to go shopping on Saturday instead.	The supervisor would appreciate Cam's flexibility and value her commitment to the job. In the future, if Cam requested a change in the work schedule, it would likely be granted, if possible.	X
Cam can tell her supervisor "no" because she is going shopping.	The supervisor would likely question Cam's commitment to the job, because shopping is viewed as something done for fun that could easily be done another time. If Cam had a commitment that was important that could not be rescheduled, she could politely tell the supervisor, "I'm sorry. I wish I could, but I have another commitment that I'm not able to reschedule."	

STRATEGY
Plan of Action: The next time Cam is asked to work a shift she was not scheduled for, she will stop and think . . . *Am I available?* If she already has plans, she will ask herself . . . *Can I change my own schedule and do it another time?* She will reply courteously to her supervisor, accepting the shift if at all possible.

SIMULATION
Practice applying the strategy:
- Carry a card with prompts for replying appropriately to the situation (if needed).
- Role-play the situation.
- Explain the strategy in your own words.

Worksheet: The SOCCSS Strategy for Teaching Hidden Curriculum (Reinke, 2018)

Purpose: Use to make the "hidden curriculum" of the workplace more explicit during "teachable moments" after a situation occurs or use the strategy to prepare students before a situation occurs.

Directions:
1. Identify the **SITUATION**. Identify the Five Ws (who, what, when, where, why).
2. List possible **OPTIONS**.
3. Consider the **CONSEQUENCES** of each option.
4. Make a **CHOICE** about the best course of action.
5. Come up with a **STRATEGY**, or a plan of action.
6. Try out the strategy in a **SIMULATION**.

SITUATION
- *Who:* _____
- *What:* _____
- *When:* _____
- *Where:* _____
- *Why:* _____

OPTION, CONSEQUENCES, CHOICE

OPTIONS	CONSEQUENCES	CHOICE

STRATEGY
Plan of Action: _____

_____

_____

SIMULATION
Practice applying the strategy:
- Carry a card with prompts for replying appropriately to the situation (if needed).
- Role-play the situation.
- Explain the strategy in your own words.

Note. Adapted from *Teaching the hidden curriculum and social communication* [Paper Presentation], by M. Reinke, Autism Society of Wisconsin Annual Conference, 2018 (https://www.autismgreaterwi.org/wp-content/uploads/2018/04/3.1_Teaching-the-Hidden-Curriculum.pdf).

ADDITIONAL RESOURCES

- How to Overcome Frustration video: https://youtu.be/kfhN1lFFwps
- Activity or chart: Things we can control vs. things we can't
- Best Autism Spectrum Disorder Resources and Learning: https://diversity.social/autism-spectrum-disorder/#3-best-autism-spectrum-disorder-resources-and-learning
- Mindreading: https://resources.autismcentreofexcellence.org/p/mindreading-all-level-bundle
- The Hidden Curriculum of Getting and Keeping a Job https://www.youtube.com/watch?v=aPVhy8QAjCI
- Autism Classroom: news and resources https://autismclassroomresources.com/hidden-curriculum-helps-students-be-employed/

CHAPTER 6

Handling Conflict on the Job

. . . .

Coworkers, Supervisors, Customers, Bullying, "Sticky Situations"

Supervisor: (during an employee meeting) *Company policy requires that you punch in ten minutes before your shift.*
Employee: Well, that's stupid! Why do we need to do that?!?

THINGS TO THINK ABOUT

- What areas of work culture are most likely to cause conflict for employees with ASD?
- What role do emotions play in conflict situations involving employees with ASD?
- What should an employee with ASD do if they are targeted or bullied at work?
- What is the best way to help people with ASD prepare for conflict in the workplace?

No one likes conflict—especially in the work environment. Conflict can cause stress and prevent an employee from doing their job efficiently. It's important to understand conflict and know how to handle it appropriately with the right person. For individuals with ASD, conflict can be particularly tricky because they often take things literally, don't interpret tone or body language well, and have trouble understanding others' perspectives. They can also be a target for bullying behavior on the job. This chapter will focus on situations that may cause conflict, emotional regulation skills, and ability to communicate and resolve a conflict appropriately.

ASD AND WORKPLACE CONFLICT

There is no doubt that conflict happens in the workplace. It can happen when people don't have the same work ethic, propose different ideas about how to complete a project, or just have very contrasting personalities. When not resolved, conflict can contribute to

. . . .

stress, decreased morale, and lower-quality work performance. It can even lead to a loss of career opportunity, or in some cases termination of employment. Individuals with ASD may have unique challenges dealing with workplace conflict because of deficits in identifying and responding appropriately to these often stressful situations. Table 6.1 includes common sources of workplace conflict and how they are a challenge for people with autism.

TABLE 6.1. Workplace Conflict and ASD Challenges

Conflict Type	Description	Challenge for People with ASD
Interdependence Conflict	When employees need to rely on one another to complete a task	Not adhering to deadlines, focusing too intensely on one small aspect of a project, work not as organized as other colleagues
Leadership Conflict	When leaders have particular expectations or communication styles	Difficulties understanding subtle cues, failure to ask questions to clarify expectations
Workplace Style Conflict	When employees have different preferences for meeting job expectations	Less interest in getting to know coworkers, sensitivity to common workplace sounds such as music or chatter
Personality Conflict	When different or opposing personalities exist in the same workplace	Inability to accept a differing opinion, talking over people, refusal to work as part of a group
Background-Based Conflict	When people's backgrounds or values influence decisions, work ethic, or communication styles	Challenges with adapting behaviors and language from an informal approach used their personal life to a formal approach that is more appropriate for the workplace

Note. Adapted from Indeed Editorial Team (2023).

It is important to point out that conflict can also exist between employees and customers. When working with the public, it is inevitable that some people will enter a place of employment frustrated, tired, or armed with a previously bad experience. Oftentimes it is up to the employee to figure out what the problem is and how to solve it, all while trying to keep the customer calm and satisfied. This can be a challenge for anyone, but it can be particularly difficult for people with ASD who struggle with reading body language and emotions from other people. When approached by a rude, unpredictable, angry, sarcastic, or flirty customer, employees with ASD might have difficulty adapting from the usual protocol to another better suited for the unique situation. For example, if a customer approaches a fast-food counter angry about an overcooked cheeseburger, demanding they get their money back, and the employee tells them that's not the rules and they should go sit down, this could escalate a conflict quickly.

To complicate matters, they might not be aware of how their own behavior is contributing to the problem, causing the conflict to grow in severity. For example, individuals with ASD may use stereotyped behaviors (aka stimming) such as random or loud vocalizations (e.g., constantly whistling or shouting "Yes!" or "I got it!") while working as a way to decrease stress. This could easily become frustrating or annoying to their coworkers. When they don't like an idea, people with ASD may criticize it honestly but severely, leading to hurt feelings. Finally, a lack of understanding of workplace norms may lead to unintentional consequences. For example, an individual with ASD may offer honest and complimentary feedback about a coworker's looks, such as "You have pretty legs" or "I wish I could go out with you." However, if unwelcome, unwanted, and/or repeated, this could be considered sexual harassment. Sexual harassment is against the law; it is defined as "unwelcome sexual advances, requests for sexual favors, and other verbal or physical harassment of a sexual nature" (U.S. Equal Employment Opportunity Commission, n.d.c.). For these reasons, it is critically important that people with ASD understand how to identify sources of conflict, regulate strong feelings related to conflict, and communicate during a conflict.

"WHAT'S THE PROBLEM?" IDENTIFYING CONFLICT

A critical first step is to increase awareness of potential scenarios where conflict is more likely to happen. Sometimes these "hot spots" are related to situations or people that are particularly challenging to the person with ASD. For example, if the individual knows they have difficulties working with others, this could be an issue if their job requires teamwork to complete a project (interdependence conflict). If the workplace culture is a social one, not attending a coworker's birthday lunch celebration might be considered rude (personality conflict). If the manager likes to hold weekly meetings to check in on employee progress, they might think the person with ASD doesn't care about their work when they act disinterested or distracted (leadership conflict).

The good news is that if the individual with ASD can identify these "conflict hot spots" before they become a conflict, they can begin to put strategies in place so they are ready to cope. See Activity 6.1 to identify "Conflict Hotspots."

ACTIVITY 6.1. What Are Your Conflict Hotspots?

A conflict "hot spot" is a situation or person that increases your chances of a conflict at work. Everyone's hot spots are different. It is important to know where your hot spots are so that you can practice making good decisions.

The following is a list of common situations that could cause conflict in the workplace. Read each scenario carefully, then decide if it is a hot spot for you by putting a checkmark in either the YES or NO column.

	Is this a hot spot for me?	
	YES	NO
Someone takes something from me without asking.		
Someone is saying something I know is wrong.		
Someone isn't following the rules.		
My schedule gets changed at the last minute.		

I'm asked to do something I don't like.
The lights in the office are too bright.
I need to work in a group to finish a project.
A customer blames me for making a mistake.
The uniform I have to wear itches my skin.
I ask for a day off and my boss tells me no.

For all of the boxes with a YES checkmark, put them in order starting with the hot spot that would be the most challenging for you.

1. _____
2. _____
3. _____
4. _____
5. _____
6. _____
7. _____
8. _____
9. _____
10. _____

Once "conflict hot spots" are uncovered, we can move on to how to solve them! One of the best ways to make a plan for handling conflict is to think through what to do when it happens. This can be accomplished by helping individuals understand basic steps for conflict resolution skills. Table 6.2 provides basic steps to conflict resolution, what's important to know at each step, and what employees with autism can do to practice.

TABLE 6.2. Conflict Resolution Steps

Step	What's Important	How to Practice
Identify the problem.	Before a plan to fix the problem can be made, both people need to understand what went wrong. Ask the other person what they think the problem is. Repeat it back to them in your own words to make sure you understand. Tell the other person what you think the problem is. Ask them if they have any questions about what you said.	Below are some common conflicts. Can you say what the problem is in one or two sentences?

Jane is looking for her clipboard. She finds it on her coworker's desk.

Mario has a great idea to share at work. During a meeting, everyone else is talking so much he doesn't get to tell them his idea. |
| Share your side. | Tell the other person what is important to you about the problem. Use a calm voice. Look the person in the eye. Do not use name calling. Do not touch the other person. | Think about a time you had a problem with someone else. In front of a mirror or someone you trust, practice calmly explaining your side. Pay attention to what your face and body look like. |

Step	What's Important	How to Practice
Understand the other person's side.	Listen carefully to what is important to the other person about the problem. Look the person in the eye. Do not interrupt them. If you feel yourself getting angry, take a deep breath and relax your muscles.	Ask someone you trust to share a story with you. Practice listening without interrupting. Ask one question about what they are saying to make sure you understand the important points.
Think about solutions.	Take time to give as many ideas as you can about what might solve the problem even if they sound silly, too difficult, or like they won't work.	Think about the following problems. Come up with at least five different ideas that might solve them:
		You ask for a day off and your boss says no.
		A customer insists you gave them the wrong change.
		A coworker is angry because you didn't finish your part of the project.
Pick the best plan for both people.	Out of all the ideas, which one will work the best for this problem? Remember that sometimes the best idea means that not everyone in the conflict gets exactly what they want. This is called compromise.	In your own words say or write a definition of "compromise."
		What is the compromise in these situations?
		You work at a fast-food restaurant. This includes taking care of the restaurant by completing a list of tasks after closing time. You think that the bathroom should be cleaned first, and your coworker believes the floors should be mopped first.
		During your shift at an ice cream parlor, you want to work the ice cream machine, but so does your coworker.
If the plan doesn't work, agree to talk again.	Sometimes even the best plans don't work forever. Agree that if this happens you will talk through things again.	Can you repeat the steps to handling conflict?

As we've discussed, conflict can happen in many different areas of the workplace. Therefore, it is important to practice. The next three activities offer common situations that might cause conflict between employees and their coworkers, bosses, and customers. First, read each conflict scenario with the individual with ASD. Be sure the context is clearly understood and that the person does not have any questions. Then review the steps to solving a conflict. Next, write down each step on the worksheet. Then review responses together, giving feedback along the way. Offer encouragement for appropriate answers. Problem-solve together any responses that were unhelpful, inaccurate, or inappropriate. Finally, invite the person with ASD to practice what they would say or do for each conflict. Practice can be done with the educator or coach, a peer, or in front of a mirror. With the person's consent, practice sessions can be audio or video recorded and played back to review strengths and areas for improvement.

See Activity 6.2 to help employees handle conflict with coworkers.

ACTIVITY 6.2. Handling Conflict with Coworkers

Nearly every job requires working successfully with other people. The following situations involve common conflicts between coworkers. Read each scenario. Using the steps for conflict resolution, write down how you would handle each problem. Review your answers with a support person.

You and your coworker are tasked with coming up with a design for a new product. When you begin working, you don't like the ideas your coworker shares. In fact, you know they won't work so you tell them their ideas are useless. When you share ideas, your coworker doesn't listen. You both start working on different designs without talking to each other.

What is the problem?

Describe how you feel or think about the problem.
How do you think the other person might feel or think about the problem?
Name three possible solutions to the problem.
Pick the best solution for both people.

What can you do if the solution doesn't work or stops working?

You are 10 minutes late for your shift because you forgot to set your alarm. When you get to the restaurant, your coworker rolls his eyes at you and tells you to hurry up because things are very busy. He looks frustrated. You think his comment is rude, so you tell him he's not the boss and stomp off to the restroom to cool off.

What is the problem?

Describe how you feel or think about the problem.
How do you think the other person might feel or think about the problem?

Name three possible solutions to the
problem.
Pick the best solution for both people.

What can you do if the solution doesn't work
or stops working?

See Activity 6.3 to help employees handle conflict with a supervisor.

ACTIVITY 6.3.   Handling Conflict with Bosses

Bosses, managers, or supervisors are responsible for making sure company policies are followed, deadlines are met, and tasks are assigned to employees. Sometimes different personality or communication styles result in conflict between bosses and employees. Read each scenario. Using the steps for conflict resolution, write down how you would handle each problem. Review your answers with a support person.

It's your first week as an airline baggage handler. You have met with your new boss, and she tells you that you should begin each day in the checked baggage area to assist with loading the planes for departure. You aren't sure where that is, so you head outside because you see people with bags. After a few minutes, she finds you and asks you why you are not inside in the baggage area like she told you. You feel embarrassed and confused.

What is the problem?

Describe how you feel or think about the
problem.
How do you think the other person might feel
or think about the problem?
Name three possible solutions to the
problem.
Pick the best solution for both people.

What can you do if the solution doesn't work
or stops working?

You love your job at the local library. However, you notice that your boss is always around when you are working. He seems to look over your shoulder when you are putting books away, checking out patrons, and using the computer. He's made a few comments about you needing extra help. You are confused because you think you are doing your job well.

What is the problem?

Describe how you feel or think about the
problem.
How do you think the other person might feel
or think about the problem?
Name three possible solutions to the
problem.
Pick the best solution for both people.

What can you do if the solution doesn't work
or stops working?

See Activity 6.4 to help employees handle conflict with customers.

ACTIVITY 6.4. Handling Conflict with Customers

For many employees, serving customers will be a big part of your job responsibilities. All
customers are different. They have different personalities, communication styles, and manners.
When working with customers, you may encounter conflict for lots of reasons such as someone
having a bad day. It's important to know how to handle this type of conflict without losing your
cool so that you can be successful at your job.

You are the manager on duty at a large movie theater. After a showing, a family approaches you
looking upset. The angry father confronts you saying the movie they saw was awful and not
worth the price of admission. He tells you this was a waste of time and demands you give them
their money back immediately.

What is the problem?

Describe how you feel or think about the
problem.
How do you think the other person might feel
or think about the problem?
Name three possible solutions to the
problem.
Pick the best solution for both people.

What can you do if the solution doesn't work
or stops working?

You own a successful flower shop. One of your most loyal customers, a wedding planner, has suddenly stopped buying arrangements from you. You decide to give him a call to ask why. He explains that although your flowers are beautiful, every time he comes into the shop you go on and on about your love of World War II. He's tried to give you some hints that he needs to get on with his busy day, but you don't seem to get the message. World War II is an intense interest for you, so you love talking about it with other people. You don't understand why he wouldn't want to spend a little extra time at the shop hearing about the famous battles.

What is the problem?

Describe how you feel or think about the problem.
How do you think the other person might feel or think about the problem?
Name three possible solutions to the problem.
Pick the best solution for both people.

What can you do if the solution doesn't work or stops working?

"BUT IT'S NOT MY FAULT!" REGULATING STRONG EMOTIONS

Since we know conflict can cause some pretty big feelings, it is important to practice emotional regulation so that the issues can be solved respectfully and professionally. Emotional regulation is "the ability to exert control over one's own emotional state. It may involve behaviors such as rethinking a challenging situation to reduce anger or anxiety, hiding visible signs of sadness or fear, or focusing on reasons to feel happy or calm" (Psychology Today, n.d.). People who regulate, or control, their emotions are able to realize when they might be too angry to have a conversation, to use strategies to help themselves calm down, and to realize what emotions are appropriate in certain situations, like work. Even if the person knows they are "right" in a situation, they still need to respond appropriately. The following resources offer great recommendations for how to stay calm during a workplace conflict (Wilson, 2022).

- Remaining-Calm-During-Conflict-I.pdf (b-cdn.net)
- Remaining-Calm-During-Conflict-II.pdf (b-cdn.net)

The best choice for managing a conflict may depend on how strongly the person experiences emotions like fear or anger that are related to the conflict. It is important for the person to understand how emotions show up in their bodies. Explaining that our bodies are always giving us information, and that if we learn to pay attention, we can know ahead of time that big feelings are on their way is a critical step for individuals with ASD to handle workplace conflict.

Activity 6.5 helps the employee to identify the emotions that often accompany conflict.

ACTIVITY 6.5. I'm Listening: Body Language

Invite the person to draw a simple outline of a body, or use this one: https://www.ormiston.org/the-link/wp-content/uploads/2018/12/Human-body-outline-80ss-Anxiety.pdf. Using different colored pencils, markers, or crayons for each feeling, ask them to color or circle areas on the body where they feel the following emotions: anger, fear, confusion, embarrassment, anxiety, and hurt. The bigger they feel the emotion, the bigger or darker the mark. The person can then be invited to describe their answers. For example, they may color the head area to indicate they get a headache during a conflict, or circle the stomach area to show they get "butterflies" during a conflict. Encourage the individual to pay attention to this "body language" as a way to know what they are feeling during a conflict. They can ask themselves "What am I feeling in my body right now?" and then "What is the best choice I can make to help solve this conflict?"

Once a person begins to realize how they are feeling during a conflict, they can explore options for managing emotions so that they don't hurt other people, say or do something inappropriate, or violate a workplace policy. Teaching employees the Three Rs: Retreat, Respond, or Request may help them remember the choices they have for managing emotions during a conflict with a coworker, boss, or customer.

Table 6.3 helps the employee to recognize and respond appropriately to the onset of emotions.

TABLE 6.3. Recognizing Emotions: Retreat, Respond, Request

What to Do	When to Do It	Why to Do It
Retreat Find a quiet and safe space to calm down.	When you notice your body telling you that you are too upset to handle a conflict right now. You might be sweating, your mind might be thinking too many things at once, or you could be crying.	To give yourself time to take care of your emotions first. Feelings, even big ones, are like waves. They may roll in strong and powerful but eventually they fade back into the ocean. Taking deep breaths or reading something you enjoy for a few minutes will allow your body to get ready to work through the conflict.
Respond Talk about the conflict with the other person. Listen, share your feelings, and work together to come up with the best solution using the conflict resolution steps.	When you are calm, your mind is clear, and you are able to listen to the other person without yelling, name calling, or interrupting.	To talk about the conflict so that a solution that works best for everyone can be chosen.

What to Do	When to Do It	Why to Do It
Request Ask for help from a supervisor or manager who can help you work through the conflict.	When you are confused, don't know what to do, or what you've tried to do to solve the conflict doesn't work. You should also ask for help if you are being bullied at work.	Sometimes conflicts are too big for one person to handle on their own. It is OK to ask for help from a boss, supervisor, or manager.

For this activity, invite the person with ASD to read each scenario. Ask them to write in which option is the best way to handle the situation based on how they are feeling. It is important for them to talk about why they made that choice. Use this opportunity to encourage appropriate answers, and correct responses that are offensive, inappropriate, or may violate workplace policy.

ACTIVITY 6.6 SHOULD I RETREAT, RESPOND, OR REQUEST?

Read each situation and write the best solution to the conflict. You should be able to tell your support person why you chose this option. Use words such as mad, scared, embarrassed, confused, or hurt to describe your feelings.

Situation 1: As part of your job, you attend a meeting with seven or eight other employees to discuss what is planned for the upcoming week. It is a time to ask questions and share ideas. However, you don't seem to get to do either because every time you open your mouth, someone interrupts or talks over you. You've told the group that sometimes it takes you a little longer to make your point, but no one seems to be listening.

Name one feeling you would have about this situation.	On a scale of 0–10, how big is this feeling? 0 = no feeling at all 10 = the biggest feeling you could have	Should you: Retreat? Respond? Request?	Explain why this is the best choice.

Situation 2: You're in the lunchroom eating your usual—a tuna sandwich and three hard-boiled eggs. A coworker at another table yells over to you that your lunch stinks and it is making him sick. The room is crowded and everyone hears him, including your boss.

Name one feeling you would have about this situation.	On a scale of 0–10, how big is this feeling? 0 = no feeling at all 10 = the biggest feeling you could have	Should you: Retreat? Respond? Request?	Explain why this is the best choice.

Situation 3: You're an auto mechanic at a small garage. One day you are alone in the shop repairing a transmission, and a customer suddenly storms in. She begins yelling at you, demanding to know when her car is going to be finished because she has to get to work. You are not the mechanic assigned to her car so you explain you don't know when the repairs will be done. She raises her voice, calls you an idiot, and tells you she is going to get you fired. Then she leaves, slamming the door to the shop.

Name one feeling you would have about this situation.	On a scale of 0–10, how big is this feeling? 0 = no feeling at all 10 = the biggest feeling you could have	Should you: Retreat? Respond? Request?	Explain why this is the best choice.

WORKING IT OUT: COMMUNICATION FOR CONFLICT RESOLUTION

It is well documented that people with ASD struggle with communication, including social communication (Santhanam & Hewitt, 2020) and process information at a slower rate (Haigh et al., 2018). According to the National Institute on Deafness and Other Communication Disorders, a division of the National Institute of Health (NIH), children with ASD utilize repetitive or rigid language, talk about narrow interests, have uneven language development, and experience difficulties understanding nonverbal communication (2020). As adults, communication challenges can show up in the workplace, especially when a conflict arises. For example, individuals with ASD may prefer to talk about their intense interest (e.g., video games) instead of working through a concern shared by a manager. They might not notice the looks of frustration on their coworkers' faces as they loudly tap their feet at their desk. Or they may repeat a learned but unhelpful phrase to a customer (e.g., "I'm sorry I can't help you.") which may escalate a conflict. Next are some basic tips for successful communication in the workplace. Asking an individual with autism to explain each strategy in their own words, and giving opportunities for practice, may help information retention. Textbox 6.1 gives tips for effective workplace communication. Each can be discussed and practiced separately through role-play, and then when mastered, become part of entire conversations.

TEXTBOX 6.1. TIPS FOR EFFECTIVE WORKPLACE COMMUNICATION

1. Look at the eyes of the person you are speaking to and when someone is speaking to you.
2. Stop what you are doing and stay in one place to make sure you can focus on what the other person is saying.
3. Say hello or good morning to coworkers when you see them. When someone leaves a room, say good-bye.
4. Keep the volume of your voice at the right place. If you speak too softly, others will not be able to hear you. If you speak too loudly, your coworkers might be startled or think you are angry.
5. Be aware of personal space. It can be uncomfortable for other people if you are too close to them. If you are too far away, they may think you don't care what they have to say. A good measure for personal space in the workplace is to stand about two arms' lengths away.
6. Show you care about the people you work with. If someone tells you they are having a bad day, you can say "I'm sorry you are having a bad day. How can I help?"
7. Use good manners. Say please and thank you. If you burp, say "Excuse me." If someone is talking to you and you didn't hear what they said, you can say, "I'm sorry. I didn't hear you; can you repeat what you just said?"
8. Remember to use professional talk at work. There are topics such as your relationship status, bathroom habits, religion, or politics that are too personal or controversial to discuss on the job. Curse words should not be used at any time.
9. Use humor in the right way. If your boss is talking about a problem, this is not the time to make a joke or a sarcastic comment. Humor should never be used to hurt people's feelings.
10. When someone tells you they are upset about something you said or did, or you know you've hurt someone's feelings, tell them you are sorry.

Even if all of these strategies are followed, conflicts may still happen. When they do it is very important that people with ASD communicate effectively. One way is to tell the other person how they feel using an "I Message." An "I Message" is a three-part script. The first part is telling the other person how they feel. The second part is sharing what the other person did that was upsetting or hurtful. The last part is asking for what they want to happen next. Here's how an "I Message" works:

I feel _____ when you _____. I'd like you to _____.

Example: I feel hurt when you leave me out of conversations. I'd like you to include me the next time the team meets to talk about our project.

Example: I feel angry when you interrupt me. Please let me finish my thoughts before you share your ideas.

Example: I feel like everyone thinks I'm stupid when you roll your eyes listening to me talk about World War II during our lunch break. This is my favorite subject, so if I go on too long, tell me directly and kindly.

If the person with autism thinks they have done or said something that started or exacerbated a conflict, this may cause stress or anxiety. It is important to teach them how to approach the other person properly so that they can work through the steps for conflict resolution. Table 6.4 provides strategies for how to begin a conversation about conflict with another person.

TABLE 6.4. Being Successful When Working Out a Conflict

Tips for Success	Why Is This Important?	Practice Makes Perfect
Be alone.	When you need to work out a conflict, it is better to talk one on one instead of in front of groups of people. If possible, talk to them in person rather than text or email so that your message does not get confused.	Would this be a good time to approach someone to work out a conflict? Why or why not? Your coworker is sitting with friends during your lunch break. Your boss is in a meeting. Your coworker is by themselves at their desk.
Be calm.	When you are calm, you can talk about the problem so that the other person understands what you are trying to say.	Do you know the differences in your facial expressions or body language when you are calm versus when you are angry? In your Job Notebook, write down three things you notice when you are calm and three things that you notice when you are angry.
Be respectful.	Being respectful during a conflict means you are upset about the problem, not the person. Even if you are very frustrated about the problem, you can still be kind as you listen to the other person's point of view. When you are acting respectfully, you will be less likely to shout, interrupt, name call, or use threats when talking to the other person.	Are these choices respectful or disrespectful when working out a conflict? Why or why not? Telling someone that's a stupid reason to be upset. Saying "I hear what you are saying" when a person is telling you why they are frustrated. Threatening to tell the boss your coworker was late to work one day. Waiting for the other person to finish talking before saying what you want to say. Walking out of the room before you have finished talking about the problem.

Tips for Success	Why Is This Important?	Practice Makes Perfect
Be focused on the facts.	Sometimes you hear about the problem from other people. This is called a rumor. Rumors may or may not be true. Rumors can make a small problem grow into a big one very quickly. When you hear something about a problem from someone else, it is important to find out the facts so that you don't accuse someone of doing something they did not do.	In the following situations, what facts do you need to help you solve the problem? How can you find out what is true? You hear from a coworker that another coworker said they don't like you. You heard people talking during break, saying that your boss was going to move you to the night shift.
Be interested in solutions.	When working through a conflict, it is easy to keep talking about the problem, especially if you are angry. It is important to talk about solutions so that the conflict is resolved.	Here are some things you can say to move the conversation from talking about the conflict to talking about the solution. Practice saying these in the mirror or with someone you trust. "What do you think should happen next?" "Do you have any ideas for how we can solve this conflict?" "Let's each give an idea that might help us work through this problem."
Be ready to compromise.	Remember, many times when solving a conflict you don't get everything you want. You sometimes have to let go of something—this is a compromise.	What would you be willing to compromise in these situations in order to solve the problem? Your boss wants you to come in two hours early on your Saturday shift. A customer wants a full refund on a meal they just ate. A coworker insists on controlling the TV in the break room.

Finally, if the conflict is chronic or complex, it is important that the person with ASD knows who to go to for help. First, if there is a resource such as an employee handbook or website that describes the workplace expectations, it is critical that the individual reads and understands the rules. This information can be reviewed with the person to determine if they fully comprehend key terminology such as harassment, dispute resolution, or discrimination (see Chapter 7 for more practice with this). Teach the person to find out who they should contact if they need help with the conflict. They should know this person's name, title, availability, and the best way to contact them. It is helpful to also have the contact information of a second person who could provide assistance if the boss or manager is not available. It should be emphasized that coming to a superior should only happen after the person has tried to solve the problem on their own, or if the concern is severe, such as in the place of workplace bullying. Activity 6.7 helps the individual identify the different roles employees play in the workplace, where to find them, and the best way to contact them.

ACTIVITY 6.7.   Who Can Help?

When you need help solving a problem at work, it is important to know who to talk to. In companies, different people handle different problems. If you know who the best person to help is, your problem will be handled more quickly and efficiently. Below are some common problems. Decide who would be the best person to share your problem with. A list of common company roles may be helpful:

Manager   Human Resources Specialist   Cashier Clerk   Office Manager

Director   Benefits Representative   Administrative Assistant   Data Entry Person

If I have a problem with **MY PAYCHECK**, I should contact:

Title of the Person:

Department:

What contact information should I have for this person? Circle all that apply:

OFFICE LOCATION   EMAIL   PHONE NUMBER   SOCIAL MEDIA CONTACT

If this person is not available, who else can I contact?

If I have a problem with **MY VACATION TIME**, I should contact:

Title of the Person:

Department:

What contact information should I have for this person? Circle all that apply:

OFFICE LOCATION   EMAIL   PHONE NUMBER   SOCIAL MEDIA CONTACT

If this person is not available, who else can I contact?

If I have a problem with **BULLYING**, I should contact:

Title of the Person:

Department:

What contact information should I have for this person? Circle all that apply:

OFFICE LOCATION   EMAIL   PHONE NUMBER   SOCIAL MEDIA CONTACT

If this person is not available, who else can I contact?

If I have a problem with **DENTAL INSURANCE**, I should contact:

Title of the Person:

Department:

What contact information should I have for this person? Circle all that apply:

OFFICE LOCATION   EMAIL   PHONE NUMBER   SOCIAL MEDIA CONTACT

If this person is not available, who else can I contact?

WHEN CONFLICT MAKES YOU A TARGET: DEALING WITH BULLYING AND HARASSMENT

When it comes to bullying and harassment, it is tempting to think it only happens to children and adolescents. Unfortunately, bullying takes place between adults including within the workplace environment. Characteristics of workplace bullying can include (1) repeated harassing behaviors that are negatively experienced by the individual, (2) single perpetrators or members of a group, (3) an imbalance of power between the target and the perpetrator of bullying, and (4) the creation of a hostile work environment (Saunders et al., 2007). A person who engages in bullying behavior is someone who "consistently bestows harm or mistreatment to other employees and brings them physical or emotional pain" (Indeed Editorial Team, 2022). Because social and communication skills are heavily relied on in the workplace (Bowman, 2020), people with ASD are at higher risk for being bullied while on the job (Cooper & Kennedy, 2021; Cooper & Mujaba, 2022). Some of this challenge deals with a lack of understanding the hidden curriculum at work, that is, "the skills we are not taught directly yet are expected to know" (Myles & Simpson, 2001, p. 279). People with ASD can struggle with interpreting body language, sarcasm, and inside jokes. They may get upset if the office plays music throughout the day and refuse to socialize with others in common areas. Sadly, it might even be the case that people with ASD are unknowingly used or manipulated by others, making them especially vulnerable targets of bullying. A recent study found that in a subsample of 96 adults with an autism diagnosis, 60% had been bullied to the point of resigning or being fired (Cooper & Kennedy, 2021). Only 3% could identify any positive aspects of their workplace (Cooper & Kennedy, 2021).

Bullying in the workplace is not only harmful, it is illegal. According to the U.S. Equal Employment Opportunity Commission (EEOC), federal law prohibits workplace harassment, which includes "unwelcome and offensive conduct that is based on race, color, national origin, sex (including pregnancy, gender identity, and sexual orientation), religion, disability, age (age 40 or older), or genetic information" (U.S. Equal Employment Opportunity Commission, n.d.b.). Not all instances are considered illegal. According to the EEOC, "for workplace harassment to be illegal, the conduct must either be severe (meaning very serious) or pervasive (meaning that it occurred frequently)" (U.S. Equal Employment Opportunity Commission, n.d.b.). Examples include abusing, excluding, or constantly criticizing an employee, screaming or using offensive language, using aggressive behavior, and undermining an employee's work (Indeed Editorial Team, 2022). Employees who feel that they have been bullied or harassed or work within a toxic environment should

- let the person who is bullying or harassing know that it is unwelcome and you want it to stop;
- tell your direct boss, supervisor, or manager; if you are uncomfortable or unable to contact your direct supervisor, you should know the next person in the chain of command to contact;
- find out if your company has an anti-harassment/bullying policy and what the process is for addressing it;

- write down each incident of bullying; include the day, time, and what happened;
- keep evidence of bullying such as emails, notes, or letters; and
- stay away from the person doing the bullying; do not bully them.

For this activity, common examples of bullying at work are listed. Using some of the previous strategies, write how you would handle each situation.

ACTIVITY 6.8. Bad Behavior: Dealing with Workplace Bullying

The following scenarios are examples of bullying in the workplace that might be particularly difficult for employees with ASD to deal with. After reading each scenario, discuss the following:

1. Describe the bullying behavior(s).
2. How do you know this was bullying?
3. How does this scenario make you feel?
4. If this happened to you, what would you do? (Answers should be safe, legal, acceptable in the workplace, and not harmful to self, others, or property.)

Scenario 1
Twenty-two-year-old Jon has ASD and works at an accounting firm. His desk cubicle is located in a large space with a dozen other coworkers. Sometimes one of his coworkers, Peter, asks Jon to tell everyone about his weekend. When Jon excitedly goes on and on about his time spent alone playing *Dungeons and Dragons*, Peter rolls his eyes and makes sarcastic comments like "Wow! Sounds like you had a rip-roaring weekend! I'm sooo jealous!" Other colleagues get the joke and start laughing. Jon thinks they want to hear more about his favorite game, so he keeps talking.

Scenario 2
Jeni is 30, lives with ASD, and is employed at a local department store. Her boss assigns her the task of folding all of the clothing items that have been disheveled after customers have looked through them. Although there are five other people working the same shift, none of them have been assigned this tedious task. While Jeni is folding, they are standing around talking or checking their phones. Jeni sees her boss in the store one day and decides to talk to her about distributing the work fairly. Jeni approaches her boss and respectfully explains her concern. As is often the case, Jeni's boss is immediately angry, telling Jeni that with her condition there's only so many tasks that she can be assigned. She tells Jeni she should be thankful she has this job there in the first place. This happens in front of Jeni's coworkers, who are standing nearby.

Scenario 3
Lukas is 27 and was diagnosed with ASD at age 15. He works as a teller at a bank. He enjoys working with his friend Joanne, who has mentored him since he started the job a year ago. Joanne often asks Lukas to help her with closing out her drawer at the end of a shift so she can gather her things. This task includes many steps to make sure the money count is accurate, and often causes Lukas to stay after his shift is over. If Joanne is going to be a few minutes late to work, she texts Lukas and asks him to cover for her until she gets there. Mornings are busy so Lukas has to work extra hard to serve all of the customers at the window. Lukas is feeling stressed from completing additional hours and tasks. He tells Joanne about this while they are eating their lunch together. She replies that they are friends, and this is how friends treat one another. She tells Lukas that she wouldn't want to be friends with someone who doesn't want to help her.

Scenario 4

Gabrielle is 28 and has ASD. She works the afternoon shift at a local post office, sorting mail in the back mailroom. Her boss, Rich, is in and out of the office throughout the week. When he's there, he frequently finds Gabrielle in the mailroom and compliments her on what she's wearing. He makes comments about how good her butt looks in her jeans, or how sexy her long hair is. A few times when he walks by Gabrielle he rubs his hand across her back, and tells her she is doing a good job. One time, he touched her upper thigh when she was putting away boxes.

As long as groups of people work together in a workplace, conflict will happen. It can be uncomfortable, frustrating, or stressful for anyone. For people with ASD who have deficits with navigating social interactions, low tolerances for change, and difficulties with communication, conflict can be particularly confusing and anxiety producing. Teaching the employee about what conflict looks like in the workplace, how they might personally experience conflict situations, and what strategies to apply to handle conflict situations are all valuable employability skills that can enhance performance and increase productivity while on the job.

CHAPTER 7

Legal Rights and Workplace Policies

··

Supervisor: We have a "zero tolerance" policy on illegal drug use. Do you have any problem with that?
Employee: What does that mean? I don't understand.

THINGS TO THINK ABOUT

- What rights do employees with ASD have under the law?
- Why is it important for employees to understand common workplace terminology?
- What resources can employees access to better understand workplace policies?
- How can employers best support their employees with ASD?

Once the job is obtained, it's important to understand workplace expectations in order to remain employed. An employee must understand their legal rights and responsibilities, as well as the policies of their particular workplace. This chapter will focus on understanding legal rights of employees with ASD, identifying common workplace terminology, describing on-the-job resources, and discussing when to self-advocate. Recommendations and resources for employers seeking to establish a more inclusive workplace environment for employees with ASD will also be provided.

LEGAL RIGHTS OF EMPLOYEES WITH ASD

Every employee has rights to protect them while on the job. The U.S. Department of Labor oversees workplace legislation with a mission to "foster, promote, and develop the welfare of the wage earners, job seekers, and retirees of the United States; improve working conditions; advance opportunities for profitable employment; and assure work-related benefits and rights" (U.S. Department of Labor, n.d.a.). Although an in-depth review of this information is beyond the scope of this chapter, the Department of Labor website includes helpful summaries pertaining to laws that protect all workers, including legislation focused on compensation, family and medical leave, and benefits

(U.S. Department of Labor, n.d.e.). People with disabilities, including employees with ASD, have particular workplace protections under the law. Here are a few that are particularly relevant:

Americans with Disabilities Act (ADA): This law "prohibits discrimination against people with disabilities in several areas, including employment, transportation, public accommodations, communications and access to state and local government programs and services" (Americans with Disabilities Act, 2020). According to ADA, employers cannot discriminate in "recruitment, hiring, promotions, training, pay, social activities, and other privileges of employment. It restricts questions that can be asked about an applicant's disability before a job offer is made, and it requires that employers make reasonable accommodations to the known physical or mental limitations of otherwise qualified individuals with disabilities, unless it results in undue hardship" (Americans with Disabilities Act). People diagnosed with autism are protected under this law. This means an employer cannot ask an applicant at an interview if they have been diagnosed with autism. Rather, the person with autism gets to choose when and whether they share their ASD diagnosis. ADA also permits employees with autism to ask for reasonable accommodations to help them be successful in carrying out their job responsibilities. This includes support for challenges like noise sensitivity, stress tolerance, and organization. The Job Accommodation Network (JAN), a service of the Department of Labor Office of Disability Employment Policy, offers ideas for accommodations based on limitation or work-related function (Job Accommodation Network, n.d.; U.S. Department of Labor, n.d.c.). For example, employees can ask for additional clocks to be added to a workspace, noise canceling headphones, or a mentor.

Section 504 of the Rehabilitation Act of 1973: This section of federal legislation states that "no qualified individual with a disability in the United States shall be excluded from, denied the benefits of, or be subjected to, discrimination under any program or activity that either receives federal financial assistance or is conducted by any executive agency or the United States Postal Service" (Autism Speaks, 2018). Discrimination is treating someone differently because of a particular reason, like having autism. Areas of workplace discrimination include "hiring, firing, pay, job assignments, promotions, layoff, training, fringe benefits, and any other term or condition of employment" (U.S. Equal Employment Opportunity Commission, n.d.a.). For example, if a person meets the qualifications of a particular job, an employer cannot refuse to hire them after becoming aware of their autism diagnosis, because this would be treating the person differently than other applicants, and therefore be considered discrimination. Similar to ADA, this law also allows employees to ask for reasonable accommodations so that they can perform the essential functions of their job.

It is important for people with ASD to understand what their rights are, including how to ask for proper accommodations, if needed. The following are some scenarios that can be used as part of a conversation to help employees recognize workplace challenges and to brainstorm possible accommodations.

See Activity 7.1 for scenarios to help employees consider appropriate accommodations in the workplace.

1. Alex has difficulty communicating orally when working in a team.
2. Samm has a sensitivity to the fabric used on the chairs in the work spaces.
3. Rae has trouble keeping track of what tasks they need to complete next.
4. Jo struggles with remembering meeting times, and is therefore often late.

Keep in mind when asking for accommodations that a person will typically need to disclose their disability status. This is a personal decision that should be carefully considered and discussed with trusted others. When asking for accommodations, it is important to be reasonable (i.e., not asking for things that are impossible to allow such as bringing a gorilla to the office), respectful (i.e., not demanding or aggressive), and professional (i.e., asking for a meeting rather than interrupting a boss's phone conversation). It may also be helpful to explain how the accommodation will help the person's job performance. The person with ASD can brainstorm and practice how to effectively ask for a workplace accommodation. For example:

"I have trouble with concentration. Having a desk in a quiet area will allow me to focus on completing tasks."

"I am sensitive to bright lights. Replacing the lightbulbs in the conference room with lower wattage bulbs will help to keep me calmer so that I can participate more in discussions."

"When I'm stressed, I struggle with stimming behaviors, such as picking my skin or pulling my hair. Allowing me to take a 10-minute break when I need one will help me cope with my anxiety so that I can continue making phone calls."

WORKPLACE POLICIES

Every workplace has a set of procedures that explain the rules and expectations for every employee. These workplace policies explain the need-to-know things, like when to arrive at work, how to take time off, what benefits and salary a workplace will provide, what is considered discrimination, and what behaviors are and are not appropriate for work. After a person is hired, most employers provide employees with a handbook that they are expected to review and sometimes sign. Therefore, it is important to know where these specific workplace policies are located. For example, is the handbook a printed manual or are the policies online? Employees should carefully read and understand the policies and procedures outlined in their handbook. If they have questions, they should identify the appropriate person they can talk to. Most workplaces have a designated human resources person or department that handles all questions related to workplace policies. Employees with autism should record who their specific human resources person is, as well as the person's email and phone number. It should be stressed that most workplace policies are not optional. Even if the employee does not agree with a reasonable or nondiscriminatory policy, they should follow it. Not doing so could risk disciplinary action or even termination of employment. The Society for Human Resource Management (SHRM) offers a robust website including an extensive glossary of commonly used terms in human resources (n.d.). Using this guide, Activity

7.2 helps the employee with ASD learn the definitions of common workplace terminology. They should not only know how to define each term, but also describe why the policy is important. Finally, they should state one way they can follow this policy while at work.

ACTIVITY 7.2.   Learning the Lingo

Use the flashcards to teach the definitions of common workplace policies. Ask the person with ASD to (1) define the policy, (2) define the policy in their own words, (3) state why the policy is important in the workplace, and (4) name one way they can be sure they are following this policy at work.

Flashcards can be printed on cardstock, cut apart, and folded on the dotted lines so that the term is on one side and the definition is on the other. Cards can be laminated if desired.

*Terms from the Society for Human Resources webpage: https://www.shrm.org/ResourcesAndTools/tools-and-samples/HR-Glossary/Pages/default.aspx

Equity	Equity is the fair treatment in access, opportunity, and advancement for all individuals.
Harassment	Harassment is defined by the Equal Employment Opportunity Commission (EEOC) as "unwelcome conduct that is based on race, color, religion, sex (including pregnancy), national origin, age (40 or older), disability or genetic information. Harassment becomes unlawful where 1) enduring the offensive conduct becomes a condition of continued employment, or 2) the conduct is severe or pervasive enough to create a work environment that a reasonable person would consider intimidating, hostile, or abusive."
Reasonable Accommodations	A reasonable accommodation, under the Americans with Disabilities Act (ADA), is a modification or adjustment of a job process or work environment that will better enable a qualified individual with a disability to perform the essential functions of a job.
Onboarding	Onboarding is the process in which new hires are integrated into an organization.
Layoff	A layoff is a separation of employment due to lack of work during periods of economic downturn or organizational restructuring. Layoffs may be permanent, or employers may implement a temporary layoff with the intention of recalling workers if circumstances allow.
Essential Job Function	Essential job functions are those job duties that an employee must be able to perform with or without reasonable accommodation.
Hostile Work Environment	A hostile work environment is created when harassing or discriminatory conduct is so severe and pervasive it interferes with an individual's ability to perform their job; creates an intimidating, offensive, threatening, or humiliating work environment; or causes a situation where a person's psychological well-being is adversely affected.
Mandatory Benefits	Mandatory benefits, also known as statutory benefits, are benefits that employers are required by law to provide to their employees. Examples include workers' compensation insurance, unemployment insurance, and, under some state and local laws, paid sick leave.

Employee Assistance Program	An employee assistance program (EAP) is a work-based intervention program designed to identify and assist employees in resolving personal problems (e.g., marital, financial, or emotional problems; family issues; substance/alcohol abuse) which may be adversely affecting the employee's performance.
Total Compensation	Total compensation refers to the complete pay package awarded to employees on an annual basis, including all direct and indirect compensation such as salary, health care and retirement benefits, incentive pay, and paid time off.

For Activity 7.3, sample employee handbooks are provided to help employees identify common workplace policies and understand why they are important and how the employees can make sure they are following them.

ACTIVITY 7.3.   Let's Do Our Policy Homework

It is important that you understand the expectations that your employer has of you. These are called workplace policies and are usually explained in a document called an employee handbook. Handbooks can sometimes be long and boring to read. But they are very important to understanding what the rules of your workplace are. Below are links to several sample employee handbooks. Choose one and see if you can find and explain some common workplace policies. Be sure to think about why they are important and how you can make sure you are making the right choices at work.

Sample Employee Handbooks
1. https://www.501commons.org/resources/tools-and-best-practices/human-resources/sample-employee-handbook-national-council-of-nonprofits
2. https://www.labordish.com/wp-content/uploads/sites/22/2014/02/12-sample-handbook_final.pdf
3. https://resources.workable.com/wp-content/uploads/2017/09/Employee-Handbook.pdf
4. https://assets.website-files.com/5c66f367239db72400eb81ed/5c7d4dbad99ee501678b3691_Employee%20Handbook%20-%20sample.pdf

Policy	What does the policy mean? Put it in your own words.	Why is this policy important?	Name one way you can be sure you are following this policy.
Work hours: attendance and punctuality			
Time off: leaves of absence, paid time off, vacations			
Workplace safety: drug and smoke free workplace, confidentiality			
Harassment, bullying, or discrimination			
Dress codes: attire, hygiene, and grooming			

Before leaving this section, it is important to talk the person with ASD through what they should do if they are ever accused of workplace misconduct. Although this situation can be incredibly stressful, especially for people who struggle with social communication, practicing what to do may increase the chances the person responds appropriately and professionally. Here is a list of situations that may be considered workplace misconduct. Review each with the person with ASD and check that they understand why this is a problem.

- Touching other people without their consent.

   Example: Tapping a coworker's shoulder when you pass by their desk.

- Saying negative or untrue things about the company.

   Example: Telling customers that they shouldn't eat in the restaurant because the soup is terrible.

- Taking anything from the office that you do not have permission to take.

   Example: Taking home supplies from the pet store you work in to give to your dog.

- Showing up late every day or not recording it truthfully.

   Example: Lying about when you actually started work on your timecard.

- Refusing to complete the tasks assigned to you.

Example: Telling your boss you will not unload the boxes because that's not your job.

- Threatening another employee or supervisor.

Example: Saying to a coworker that if they don't go out with you, you'll tell their supervisor about personal pictures they posted to a social media page.

It may also be worthwhile to explain that there are some topics that should not be discussed in the workplace because they are too controversial, offensive, or personal. Some of these include politics, religion, bodily functions, other employees' performances, inappropriate jokes, racial slurs, and uninvited personal questions. For example, it is never a good idea to ask someone if they are pregnant, gossip about who got a raise and who didn't, or who you voted for in the last election. The person with ASD might not think these questions are a big deal, but explain that other people might perceive things differently than they do. A situation that is not handled properly can cause problems such as people reporting to their manager being uncomfortable or angry about something the person with ASD has said or done. This could lead to negative consequences, such as being written up, becoming part of a workplace investigation, or even being fired.

Steps to Take If You Are Accused of Workplace Misconduct

- Stay calm. Do not respond until you are sure you are calm and focused.
- Understand what you are being accused of. You have a right to know what the nature of the complaint is. Ask questions if you do not understand.
- Provide your side of the story, including any evidence you have to support what you are saying. This includes documents such as time cards, logs, records, and accounts. You should only discuss the facts, not your opinion of the situation or other people.
- Know what the next steps are in the process and when they are taking place.
- If necessary, ask for an advocate or legal representation.
- If you know who has made the accusation against you, you should never retaliate against them. Retaliation happens when someone tries to "get someone back" if that person has said or done something mean, hurtful, or untrue. Examples of retaliation include talking to the accuser after you've been told not to, telling other people how horrible the other person is, sending nasty text messages or emails, or threatening the other person.

Self-Advocacy: When to Speak Up

There are situations in which an employee with ASD may need to address a concern they have with their employment. Problems may vary, but can include issues with accommodations, bullying or harassment, or questions related to policies or job performance. Since people with ASD struggle with communicating in complex social interactions, this may be particularly difficult, resulting in the concerns getting worse and impacting the person's ability to complete their assigned tasks. It is important during job preparation that people with ASD are taught self-advocacy skills. Self-advocacy in the workplace involves knowing who to approach and how to approach them about resolving a job-related problem using understanding and negotiation skills (Shore, 2004). A person can choose to self-advocate to help another person understand a concern, to improve a workplace condition, or to ensure a policy is being followed. When self-advocating, it is important to remember some key points:

- Increase the person's awareness of how their autism diagnosis may impact them, specifically in the workplace. If they have access to their diagnostic paperwork, review key information with them. This will help the person better understand what they may need during the workday to be successful.
- Remind that person that self-advocating often involves disclosing that they have autism. Together, write the pros and cons of telling a boss they live with ASD. For example, a pro might be that their boss may better understand why they prefer to eat lunch in their office. A con might include the boss thinking they can't share concerns with the person because the boss fears they won't be able to handle criticism.
- When self-advocating, it is important to use an assertive rather than an aggressive communication style. When communicating assertively, a person looks the other person in the eyes and speaks calmly. They explain what the problem is using facts rather than opinions. They state what they think and how they feel about the situation. They keep the conversation focused on work. Finally, they clearly ask for what they want. In contrast, communicating aggressively means the person may yell, use inappropriate language, accuse or blame the other person, or have no clear solutions for what they want. Aggressive communication may make the other person feel uncomfortable, disrespected, or angry.

For more information about self-advocacy and autism, the Autistic Self Advocacy Network has offered the following resource: https://www.autisticadvocacy.org/resources/. Additionally, the Self Advocates Becoming Empowered (SABE) organization provides resources for self-advocacy groups, webinars, and other resources for people with disabilities: https://sabeusa.org/resources/. Finally, this article discusses strategies for how to advocate for accommodations: https://autism.org/autism-workplace-accomodations/.

Now that we know what self-advocacy is and why it's important, let's practice strengthening self-advocacy skills. For this activity, read each scenario and use the script template provided to demonstrate the skills needed to assertively communicate a concern to a boss or coworker. Invite the person with ASD to say their responses out loud to you, a peer, or even a mirror.

See Activity 7.4 to help employees learn to self-advocate appropriately.

ACTIVITY 7.4. Speaking Up the Right Way

Read each situation. Think about how you might apply the assertiveness skills discussed in Chapter 7 to self-advocacy. Use the script provided to practice being clear, calm, and respectful. Ask a trusted person for their feedback.

Scenario 1: You have been employed by your company for three years. During this time, you have been told by your boss that you are doing a good job. Every time your performance is reviewed, you get high scores. However, you have never received a raise. You decide to talk to your boss and ask for a small increase in your pay.

Explain what the problem is.
Say what you think or feel about how
    the problem is affecting you.
Clearly ask for what you want.

Scenario 2: You always have to work on Christmas day. Your family has a big celebration that you have to miss every year. You find out that other coworkers never have to work on this holiday.

Explain what the problem is.
Say what you think or feel about how
    the problem is affecting you.
Clearly ask for what you want.

Scenario 3: As you walk by your boss's office, you overhear her telling a coworker that you have autism. You never gave your boss permission to share this, because you didn't want your coworkers to know about your diagnosis.

Explain what the problem is.
Say what you think or feel about how
    the problem is affecting you.
Clearly ask for what you want.

A Recipe for Success: Recommendations for Employers

Although it is best if employees with ASD learn their rights and responsibilities, it can also be helpful if employers are able to create an environment to help their employees thrive. Employers can adhere to requests for accommodations, provide some structure to the workday, use clear and direct communication, and increase their knowledge of ASD through professional development (Bowman, 2020). They can also model inclusion in the workplace because as participants in one study reported, up to 60% had resigned or been terminated from a position due to issues related to bullying (Bowman, 2020; Cooper & Kennedy, 2021). Educating the entire workplace on bullying behaviors and how to avoid a toxic work environment can go a long way in creating a safe and comfortable space for everyone. Employees with ASD can also be provided with a mentor or coach who can help them navigate the "hidden curriculum." This person does not have to be an expert in autism, but rather they can serve as a guide to explain workplace norms and to answer questions. Organizational tools such as checklists, meeting minutes, and agendas can be made available to provide clarity and reduce anxiety about what is expected. Outlining the steps to particular job tasks or creating a video showing the proper way to carry out a specific function (e.g., how to use the register) may help the person fully understand what is expected of them (Cooper & Mujtabe, 2022). People with autism can benefit from regular check-ins with their supervisor to get feedback on their performance. Scheduling short but consistent meetings will help ensure that the employee is on track and avoid potential problems. Finally, allowing for nonverbal communication, such as text or email, may help increase dialogue between the employee, coworkers, and the boss (Cooper & Mujtabe, 2022).

If a person feels comfortable, they can ask their supervisor or boss about their experience with working with an employee on the spectrum. An open dialogue about what the employee needs to be successful on the job, what resources are available for support, and who to contact when there are problems is a great starting place. A support person may help the employee develop and role-play a script to increase their comfort level. Here is a sample script for an employee who has chosen to disclose their disability status.

> Thank you for meeting with me today. As you know, I have autism, and I was hoping we could talk about how my specific symptoms impact my workday, and how we can work together to come up with some strategies to help me be successful. My job is important to me, and I want to make sure that I am doing my best every day.

Here are a few sample questions the person might choose to ask during this conversation:

1. How familiar are you with working with people with autism?
2. Would you be comfortable with me sharing some resources with you about autism and the workplace?
3. Can we collaborate on developing accommodations to support my productivity?
4. If either of us has a concern, what is the best way to communicate with each other?

Be sure to listen, avoid interrupting, and thank the employer for their time. If strategies are developed, the person should keep their commitment.

People with ASD can bring tremendous value to the workplace. They can offer great attention to detail, reliability, honesty, and out-of-the-box thinking that can support the health and growth of a company. Teaching employees to know their rights, to understand the importance of workplace policies, and to speak up when needed will reinforce their job success. Likewise, collaborating with and educating employers about how they can support their employees in the workplace can increase both morale and productivity. This is a win for the entire organization.

ADDITIONAL RESOURCES

The following are some resources that employers can be referred to for more information.

- UDS Foundation: Autism in the Workplace: How to Accommodate Adults with Autism at Work: https:www.udservices.org/employees-with-autism/
- National Autistic Society: Employing Autistic People: A Guide for Employers: https://www.autism.org.uk/advice-and-guidance/topics/employment/employing -autistic-people/employers
- Monster.com: How to Support Employees with Autism in the Workplace: https:// hiring.monster.com/resources/workforce-management/diversity-in-the-work place/hiring-autistic-job-candidates/

CHAPTER 8

Case Studies

$\cdots\cdots\cdots\cdots\cdots\cdots\cdots\cdots\cdots\cdots\cdots\cdots\cdots\cdots\cdots\cdots\cdots\cdots\cdots\cdots\cdots\cdots\cdots\cdots\cdots\cdots\cdots\cdots$

In this final chapter, case studies are presented to encourage discussion and problem solving among individuals supporting the career development of employees with ASD. Cases will highlight specific aspects of the job search and preparation process that are particularly challenging for the individual with ASD. During professional development or case conference discussion, read each case. Apply concepts discussed in previous chapters to answer the questions below. Cases can be adapted to fit the individual needs of the employees.

CASE STUDY QUESTIONS

1. What common traits of individuals with ASD are evident in the case?
2. What mistakes, errors, or poor choices were made by the individual with ASD in the situation?
3. What assumptions might be made by a neurotypical supervisor, coworker, or customer about the individual with ASD?
4. What feedback would be helpful to the individual with ASD, and what is the best way to provide it?
5. What strategies could be used by a teacher or mentor to support the individual with ASD to navigate the situation more successfully in the future?

CASE STUDY 8.1: QUINN

Mr. Johnson is a special educator who is working on employability skills with his students. He has a colleague, Ms. Yin, from the community, who agrees to work with coaching students on interviewing skills. They have been working on interview skills for four weeks and this week Ms. Yin will conduct mock interviews. Ms. Yin approaches Quinn, a student in the class, extending her hand to shake, as if they are meeting for an interview. Quinn looks at her, clearly puzzled. *"But you know me"* he says. Ms. Yin responds, *"Yes, but we are practicing interviewing skills today, remember?"*

Quinn is invited to take a seat across from Ms. Yin.

"Hello, Quinn. How are you doing today? Have you been waiting long?"

"Not great. I threw up before school and I have been waiting for 15 minutes for you to arrive."

"Why are you interested in this job?"

"Because I need a job."

"What are your strengths?"

"I'm good at video games."

"How would those strengths assist you in this job?"

No response.

"How are you working in a group?"

No response.

As the interview wraps up . . .

"Do you have any questions for me?"

"No."

CASE STUDY 8.2: JOSEPH

Joseph is a 20-year-old male with ASD. Joseph loves anything to do with Japanese culture. Joseph is very skilled in computer technology. He loves gaming, particularly with Japanese samurai warriors, but he is also good at troubleshooting. When something goes wrong with the technology, Joseph is able to figure out issues with computer program glitches and fix them quickly. Joseph is very outgoing and congenial but loves to talk incessantly about his interests. He has few friends. Those friends he has are from his gaming community or social media venues who share his interests, and he interacts with them virtually. In high school, his teachers indulged his interests, even allowing him to wear traditional kimonos to class. James has never been employed. He is currently in a college-based transition program that is preparing him for competitive employment.

Joseph is asked to attend a mock interview for a position in customer service. He attends the interview dressed in a kimono. The interviewer comments that his costume is interesting. Joseph immediately sits down and begins telling the interviewer the origins of the costume and the customs that are associated with the kimono. The interviewer begins to ask typical questions:

"Tell me about your educational background."

"I am a self-learned man. I study everything there is on the internet and watch the Discovery Channel."

"What are the skills that enable you to do the job?"

"I'm very smart, sensei. I am good at playing Japanese Warrior *and have made it to the tenth level."*

"What do you think about the 'customer is always right'?"

"They aren't!"

"Why do you want the job?"

"Ha! To make money."

"If asked to work an extra shift, would you be available?"

"No."

CASE STUDY 8.3: MARY

Mary worked in the produce section at a local grocery store. As a promotion, the bakery displayed a sign that read, "Free Cookies." Mary loved cookies so she took five. She overheard the customers saying, "What a pig!" Then her boss came and told her customers had complained about her and that they would be charging her for the cookies. She didn't understand why anyone would have a problem with her taking free cookies since that is what the sign said. Mary didn't understand that she should not take them as an employee, nor should she take multiple cookies.

CASE STUDY 8.4: ALEXANDER

Alexander is a 19-year-old individual diagnosed with high-functioning autism spectrum disorder. He works in the maintenance department at a busy family campground. An important part of his job is raking and disposing of debris around the camp's beach area. During the day, this area can be crowded with people swimming, relaxing by the water, and playing basketball. One day, while Alexander is working on the beach, a group of adults, standing near the water, block his way to a pile of sticks and leaves. The following exchange takes place:

Alexander: *"You're in my way!"* (yelling)
Camper: *"Excuse me?"*
Alexander: *"I said, you're in my way. Move."*
Camper: *"You gotta be kidding me. Just go around us."*
Alexander: *"No. I have to go THIS way. MOVE!"*
Camper: *"You are being very rude."*
Alexander: *"No I'm not. You're rude."*

CASE STUDY 8.5: SHAY

Shay, a 25-year-old woman, was diagnosed with autism at age eight. She struggles with social interactions and in-person communication. She is employed as a paralegal at a moderately sized law firm. Among her responsibilities are researching case law and providing her findings to the firm's partners to assist them with court preparation. In the office, Shay wears earphones to block out excess noise. She relies on watching videos on her iPhone to help her de-stress throughout the day. When she is working at her computer, she often has several tabs open to monitor her status on her favorite game and to chat with other players. Several of the partners have noticed that every time they walk by her office, Shay seems to be playing video games instead of working. In meetings, Shay looks down at her phone most of the time. When someone tries to get her attention, her headphones block out their voices. Shay's direct supervisor is concerned about her performance and schedules a meeting to discuss these issues. During the meeting,

Shay does not look her supervisor in the eye, interrupts, and argues with him when he suggests things that need to change.

CASE STUDY 8.6: COLLIN

Collin works at a restaurant bar at a marina. Collin buses tables and washes dishes. Collin wears earphones to reduce noise and stress, which he discloses to his boss. Often coworkers feel he is "rude" because he ignores them when they speak to him. When he does talk, he gives short answers. During Karaoke Night, the bar is busy and loud. A patron knocks over a glass of water, and Collin is asked to clean it up. Collin comments to the customer, "You should be more careful." A coworker overhears and tells Collin, "You shouldn't speak that way to customers." Collin ignores him. The manager is notified and sends him home for the evening. The next day, Collin quits.

CASE STUDY 8.7: MELANIE

Melanie works in the office at a school. Melanie de-stresses by talking through her upcoming events and problems aloud, while pacing. Most people think she is talking on the phone. Melanie is very pleasant and social; however, she rarely goes to the break room. She prefers the routine of eating at her desk and de-stressing in the hallway during lunchtime. Parents and teachers are uncomfortable seeing an adult pace up and down the hallway talking to themselves. Students become distracted when Melanie is walking in the hallway in front of their classrooms.

References

··

Americans with Disabilities Act. (2020). *Guide to disability rights laws.* https://www.ada.gov/resources/disability-rights-guide/

Arter, P., Brown, T. H., Barna, J., Law, M., Fidiam, R., Fruehan, A., & Daquila, J. (2021). You're hired! *TEACHING Exceptional Children, 54*(6), 440–448. https://doi.org/10.1177/00400599211027299

Ashkam, A. V. (2022, April 8). "Theory of Mind" in autism: A research field reborn. *Autism Spectrum News.* https://www.spectrumnews.org/features/deep-dive/theory-of-mind-in-autism-a-research-field-reborn/

Aspy, R., & Grossman, B. (2007). *Underlying characteristics checklist (UCC-CL).* https://autisminternetmodules.org/storage/ocali-ims-sites/ocali-ims-aim/documents/ElleCaseStudy.pdf

Autism Society. (2019). *Employment.* https://www.autism-society.org/living-with-autism/autism-through-the-lifespan/adulthood/employment.

Autism Speaks. (2018). *My employment rights: Employment tool kit.* https://www.autismspeaks.org/tool-kit-excerpt/my-employment-rights

Bernick, M. S., & Holden, R. (2015). *The Autism Job Club.* Skyhorse Publishing.

Blessing, C. (2001). *Infusing a person centered approach into transition planning for students with developmental disabilities.* https://ecommons.cornell.edu/bitstream/handle/1813/89848/T8_PDF1.pdf?sequence=1&isAllowed=

Bolles, R. N. (2017). *What color is your parachute? 2017: A practical manual for job-hunters and career-changers.* Ten Speed Press.

Bonaccio, S., Connelly, C. E., Gellatly, I. R., Jetha, A., & Martin Ginis, K. A. (2020). The participation of people with disabilities in the workplace across the employment cycle: Employer concerns and research evidence. *Journal of Business and Psychology, 35*(2), 135–158. https://doi.org/10.1007/s10869-018-9602-5

Bowman, A. D. (2020). What we know about employers' perspectives on successfully integrating adults with autism spectrum disorders in the workplace. *International Journal of Psychiatric Research, 3*(1), 1–4. http://dx.doi.org/10.33425/2641-4317.1054

Bureau of Labor and Statistics. (2022, February 24). *Persons with a disability: Labor force characteristics—2021* [Press release]. https://www.bls.gov/news.release/disabl.nr0.htm

Burke, S. L., Bresnahan, T., Li, T., Epnere, K., Rizzo, A., Partin, M., Ahlness, R. M., & Trimmer, M. (2018). Using virtual interactive training agents (ViTA) with adults with autism and other developmental disabilities. *Journal of Autism and Developmental Disorders, 48*(3), 905–912. https://doi.org/10.1007/s10803-017-3374-z

Buron, K. D., & Wolfberg, P. J. (2008). *Learners on the autism spectrum: Preparing highly qualified educators.* AAPC Publishing.

Buron, K. D., Wolfberg, P. J. (2014). *Learners on the autism spectrum: Preparing highly qualified educators and related practitioners* (2nd ed.). AAPC Publishing.

Center on Transition Innovations. (2020). *Workplace readiness toolkit: Practicing employment skills at home.* Virginia Commonwealth University. https://centerontransition.org/transition/Employment/workplacereadinessskills.html

Centers for Disease Control and Prevention (CDC). (2022a, April 6). *Autism spectrum disorder in teenagers & adults.* https://www.cdc.gov/ncbddd/autism/autism-spectrum-disorder-in-teenagers-adults.html

··

Centers for Disease Control and Prevention (CDC). (2022b, April 7). *Key findings: CDC releases first estimates of the number of adults living with autism spectrum disorder in the United States.* https://www.cdc.gov/ncbddd/autism/features/adults-living-with-autism-spectrum-disorder.html

Chen, C., Lee, I., & Lin, L. (2015). Augmented reality-based self-facial modeling to promote the emotional expression and social skills of adolescents with autism spectrum disorders. *Research in Developmental Disabilities, 36C*, 396–403. https://doi.org/10.1016/j.ridd.2014.10.015

Ciampi, M. (2018). *Disclosing autism on the job? Yes or no?* College Central. https://researchautism.org/disclosing-autism-on-the-job-yes-or-no/

Cooper, A. A., & Mujaba, B. G. (2022). Assessment of workplace discrimination against individuals with autism spectrum disorder (ASD). *SocioEconomic Challenges, 6*(2), 19–28. https://doi.org/10.21272/sec.6(2)

Cooper, R., & Kennedy, C. (2021). Autistic voices from the workplace. *Advances in Autism, 7*(1), 73–85. https://doi.org/10.1108/AIA-09-2019-0031

Dean, E. E., Shogren, K. A., Wehmeyer, M. L., Almire, B., & Mellenbruch, R. (2019). Career design and development for adults with intellectual disability: A program evaluation. *Advances in Neurodevelopmental Disorders, 3*(2), 111–118. https://doi.org/10.1007/s41252-018-0080-6

DO-IT, University of Washington. (2022). *Why should a company hire a person with a disability?* https://www.washington.edu/doit/why-should-company-hire-person-disability

Dreaver, J., Thompson, C., Girdler, S., Adolfsson, M., Black, M. H., & Falkmer, M. (2019). Success factors enabling employment for adults on the autism spectrum from employers' perspective. *Journal of Autism and Developmental Disorders, 50*(5), 1657–1667. https://doi.org/10.1007/s10803-019-03923-3

Falvey, M. A., Forest, M., Pearpoint, J., & Rosenberg, R. L. (2020). *All my life's a circle: Using the tools: Circles, maps & paths.* Inclusion Press.

Fast, Y. (2004). *Employment for individuals with Asperger Syndrome or non-verbal learning disability: Stories and strategies.* Jessica Kingsley.

Fast, Y. (2012). Career planning for people on the autism spectrum. *Autism Spectrum News.* https://www.autismspectrumnews.org/career-planning-for-people-on-the-spectrum/

GatewaytoSD. (2011, November 4). *Using lifebooks for self-advocacy* [Video]. YouTube. https://www.youtube.com/watch?v=cKZOx6ghGgg

Greenwald, M. (2018, August 1). 40 things you should never say to your boss: Especially if your goal is to rise the ranks. *BestLife.* https://bestlifeonline.com/never-say-to-boss/

Haigh, S. M., Walsh, J. A., Mazefsky, C. A., Minshew, N. J., & Eack, S. M. (2018). Processing speed is impaired in adults with Autism Spectrum Disorder, and relates to social communication abilities. *Journal of Autism and Developmental Disorders, 48*(8), 2653–2662. https://doi.org/10.1007%2Fs10803-018-3515-z

Hall, J., Morgan, R. L., & Salzberg, C. L. (2014). Job-preference and job-matching assessment results and their association with job performance and satisfaction among adults with developmental disabilities. *Education and Training in Autism and Developmental Disabilities, 49*(2), 301–312.

Hayes, G. R., Custodio, V. E., Haimson, O. L., Nguyen, K., Ringland, K. E., Ulgado, R. R., Waterhouse, A., & Weiner, R. (2015). Mobile video modeling for employment interviews for individuals with autism. *Journal of Vocational Rehabilitation, 43*(3), 275–287. https://doi.org/10.3233/jvr-150775

Hayes, M., & Muldoon, M. (2013). *Students Transitioning to Adult Roles (STAR) Person Centered Planning (PCP).* Transition and Postsecondary Programs for Students with Intellectual Disabilities into Higher Education (TPSID) grant awarded to the Florida Consortium on Postsecondary Education and Disabilities from the U.S. Department of Education, Office of Postsecondary Education from 2010–2015. #CFDA 84.407A, P407A100034.

Hendricks, D. (2010). Employment and adults with autism spectrum disorders: Challenges and strategies for success. *Journal of Vocational Rehabilitation, 32*, 125–134. https://doi.org/10.3233/JVR-2010-0502.

Iacomini, S., Berardo, F., Cavallini, F., & Dipace, A. (2021). Assessment tools for the career planning of adolescents and adults with neurodevelopmental disorders: A systematic review. *Journal of Clinical & Developmental Psychology, 3*(3), 34–55. https://doi.org/https://doi.org/10.13129/2612-4033/0110-3200

Indeed Editorial Team. (2022). *How to manage workplace bullying (with examples)*. Indeed. https://www.indeed.com/career-advice/career-development/workplace-bully

Indeed Editorial Team. (2023). *5 examples of conflict in the workplace (with solutions)*. Indeed. https://au.indeed.com/career-advice/career-development/examples-of-conflict-in-the-workplace

Individuals with Disabilities Education Improvement Act (IDEA), H.R. 1350, 108th Congress (2004).

Institute for Educational Leadership. (2018). *Guideposts for success: Lesson plans and activities; Lesson 23: Goal setting begins with a dream*. http://www.ncwd-youth.info/wp-content/uploads/2018/02/Guideposts-Lesson-23.pdf

Job Accommodation Network (n.d.). *Autism spectrum: Accommodation and compliance*. https://www.askjan.org/disabilities/Autism-Spectrum.cfm

Jordan, M. (n.d.). *Workplace accommodation: tips*. Autism Research Institute. https://www.autism.org/autism-workplace-accommodations/

Kim, C. (2014). *Nerdy, shy, and socially inappropriate: A user guide to an Asperger life*. Jessica Kingsley.

Kumazaki, H., Muramatsu, T., Yoshikawa, Y., Matsumoto, Y., Ishiguro, H., Mimura, M., & Kikuchi, M. (2019). Role-play-based guidance for job interviews using an android robot for individuals with autism spectrum disorders. *Frontiers in Psychiatry, 10*, Article 239. https://doi.org/10.3389/fpsyt.2019.00239

LaRue, R. H., Maraventano, J. C., Budge, J. L., & Frischmann, T. (2019). *Matching vocational aptitude and employment choice for adolescents and adults with ASD*. https://doi.org/10.1007/s40617-019-00398-7

LaRue, R. H., Maraventano, J. C., Budge, J. L., & Frischmann, T. (2020). *Skill-based vocational assessment*. PsycTESTS Dataset. https://doi.org/10.1037/t78457-000

Levy, M., Gentry, D., & Klesges, L. M. (2015). Innovations in public health education: Promoting professional development and a culture of health. *American Journal of Public Health, 105*(S1). https://doi.org/10.2105/ajph.2014.302351

Mawhood, L., & Howlin, P. (1999). The outcome of a supported employment scheme for high-functioning adults with autism or Asperger syndrome. *Autism, 3*(3), 229–254. https://doi.org/10.1177/1362361399003003003

Minot, D. (2022, January 21). Career planning for people on the autism spectrum. *Autism Spectrum News*. https://autismspectrumnews.org/career-planning-for-people-on-the-autism-spectrum/

Morgan, L., Leatzow, A., Clark, S., & Siller, M. (2014). Interview skills for adults with autism spectrum disorder: A pilot randomized controlled trial. *Journal of Autism and Developmental Disorders, 44*(9), 2290–2300. https://doi.org/10.1007/s10803-014-2100-3

Morgan, R. L. (2008). Job matching: Development and evaluation of a web-based instrument to assess degree of match among employment preferences. *Journal of Vocational Rehabilitation, 29*(1), 29–38.

Morningstar, M., & Clavenna-Deane, B. (2018). *Your complete guide to transition planning and services*. Paul H. Brookes.

Morningstar, M. E., Gaumer-Erickson, A., Lattin, D., & Wilkerson, D. (2012). *Enhancing employment outcomes for youth with disabilities*. Center for Research on Learning, University of Kansas. https://transitioncoalition.org/

Munandar, V. D., Morningstar, M. E., & Carlson, S. R. (2020). A systematic literature review of video-based interventions to improve integrated competitive employment skills among youth and adults with autism spectrum disorder. *Journal of Vocational Rehabilitation, 53*(1), 29–41. https://doi.org/10.3233/jvr-201083

Myles, B. S., Endow, J., & Mayfield, M. (2013). *The hidden curriculum of getting and keeping a job: Navigating the social landscape of employment*. AAPC Publishing.

Myles, B. S., & Simpson, R. L. (2001). Understanding the hidden curriculum: An essential social skill for children and youth with Asperger's syndrome. *Intervention in School and Clinic, 36*(5), 279–286. https://doi.org/10.1177%2F105345120103600504

National Institute on Deafness and Other Communication Disorders. (2020). *Autism spectrum disorder: Communication problems in children*. https://www.nidcd.nih.gov/health/autism-spectrum-disorder-communication-problems-children#3

Oliver, V. (2021). 10 Common job interview questions and how to answer them. *Harvard Business Review*. https://hbr.org/2021/11/10-common-job-interview-questions-and-how-to-answer-them

Peterson, T. (2023). *100 Interview questions*. Monster. https://www.monster.com/career-advice/article/100-potential-interview-questions

Psychology Today. (2022). Emotion regulation. *Psychology Today*. https://www.psychologytoday.com/us/basics/emotion-regulation

Reichow, B., & Volkmar, F. R. (2010). Social skills interventions for individuals with autism: Evaluation for evidence-based practices within a best evidence synthesis framework. *Journal of Autism and Developmental Disorders, 40*, 149–166. https://doi.org/10.1007/s10803-009-0842-0

Reinke, M. (2018, April 18–21). *Teaching the hidden curriculum and social communication*. [Paper Presentation]. Autism Society of Wisconsin Annual Conference, Wisconsin Dells, WI. https://www.autismgreaterwi.org/wp-content/uploads/2018/04/3.1_Teaching-the-Hidden-Curriculum.pdf

Roberts, K., DeQuinzio, J. A., Taylor, B. A., & Petroski, J. (2021). Using behavioral skills training to teach interview skills to young adults with autism. *Journal of Behavioral Education, 30*(4), 664–683. https://doi.org/10.1007/s10864-020-09389-z

Roux, A. M., Rast, J. E., Anderson, K. A., & Shattuck, P. T. (2017). *National autism indicators report: Developmental disability services and outcomes in adulthood*. Life Course Outcomes Program, A. J. Drexel Autism Institute, Drexel University.

Sanford, C., Newman, L., Wagner, M., Cameto, R., Knokey, A.-M., & Shaver, D. (2011). *The post high school outcomes of young adults with disabilities up to 6 years after high school. Key findings From the National Longitudinal Transition Study-2 (NLTS2) (NCSER 2011–3004)*. SRI International.

Santhanam, S. P., & Hewitt, L. E. (2020). Perspectives on adults with autism on social communication intervention. *Communication Disorders Quarterly, 42*(3), 156–165. https://doi.org/10.1177/1525740120905501

Saunders, P., Huynh, A., & Goodman-Delahunty, J. (2007). Defining workplace bullying behaviour: Professional lay definitions of workplace bullying. *Journal of Law and Psychiatry, 30*, 340–354.

Shogren, K. A., Wehmeyer, M. L., Palmer, S. B., & Paek, Y. (2013). Exploring personal and school environment characteristics that predict self-determination. *Exceptionality, 21*(3), 147–157. https://doi.org/10.1080/09362835.2013.802231

Shore, S. M. (2004). *Self advocacy*. Autism Research Institute. https://www.autism.org/self-advocacy/

Smith, M. J., Fleming, M. F., Wright, M. A., Losh, M., Humm, L. B., Olsen, D., & Bell, M. D. (2015). Brief report: Vocational outcomes for young adults with autism spectrum disorders at six months after virtual reality job interview training. *Journal of Autism and Developmental Disorders, 45*(10), 3364–3369. https://doi.org/10.1007/s10803-015-2470-1

Smith, M. J., Pinto, R. M., Dawalt, L., Smith, J. D., Sherwood, K., Miles, R., Taylor, J., Hume, K., Dawkins, T., Baker-Ericzén, M., Frazier, T., Humm, L., & Steacy, C. (2020). Using community-engaged methods to adapt virtual reality job-interview training for transition-age youth on the autism spectrum. *Research in Autism Spectrum Disorders, 71*, 101498. https://doi.org/10.1016/j.rasd.2019.101498

Society for Human Resources Management. (n.d.). *HR glossary*. https://www.shrm.org/ResourcesandTools/toolsandsamples/HR-Glossary/Pages/default.aspx

Solomon, C. (2020). Autism and employment: Implications for employers and adults with ASD. *Journal of Autism and Developmental Disorders, 50*(11), 4209–4217. https://doi.org/10.1007/s10803-020-04537-w

Sulaimani, M., & Gut, D. (2019). Hidden curriculum in a special education context: The case for individuals with autism. *Journal of Educational Research and Practice, 9*(1), 30–39. https://doi.org/10.5590/JERAP.2019.09.1.03

U.S. Department of Labor. (n.d.a.). *About us*. https://www.dol.gov/general/aboutdol

U.S. Department of Labor. (n.d.b.). *Americans with disabilities act*. https://www.dol.gov/general/topic/disability/ada

U.S. Department of Labor. (n.d.c.). *Office of Disability Employment Policy*. www.dol.gov/agencies/odep

U.S. Department of Labor. (n.d.d.) *Soft skills to pay the bills*. https://www.dol.gov/agencies/odep/program-areas/individuals/youth/transition/soft-skills

U.S. Department of Labor (n.d.e.). *Summary of major laws of the Department of Labor*. https://www.dol.gov/general/aboutdol/majorlaws

U.S. Equal Employment Opportunity Commission. (n.d.a.). *Disability discrimination and employment decisions*. https://www.eeoc.gov/disability-discrimination-and-employment-decisions.

U.S. Equal Employment Opportunity Commission. (n.d.b.). *Harassment: FAQs*. Harassment—FAQs | U.S. Equal Employment Opportunity Commission (eeoc.gov)

U.S. Equal Employment Opportunity Commission. (n.d.c.). *Sexual harassment*. https://www.eeoc.gov/sexual-harassment

Wehmeyer, M. L. (2005). Self-determination and individuals with severe disabilities: Re-examining meanings and misinterpretations. *Research and Practice for Persons with Severe Disabilities, 30*(3), 113–120.

Wehmeyer, M. L., & Palmer, S. B. (2003). Adult outcomes for students with cognitive disabilities three years after high school: The impact of self-determination. *Education and Training in Developmental Disabilities, 38*(2), 131–144.

West Sussex County Council. (2017). *Person centered planning*. https://schools.local-offer.org/childs-journey/paths-bella/

Whetzel, M. (2014). Interviewing tips for applicants with autism spectrum disorder (ASD). *Journal of Vocational Rehabilitation, 40*(2), 155–159. https://doi.org/10.3233/JVR-140668

Wilson, C. R. (2022). 14 conflict resolution strategies for the workplace. *Positivepsychology.com.* 14 Conflict Resolution Strategies for the Workplace (positivepsychology.com).

Zielin, L. (2012). *Make things happen: The key to networking for teens*. ReadHowYouWant.

Index

....

hidden curriculum, 79–80; and match, 29–30; and relevance, 42

child care skills, proficiency levels, 51*t*

choice, and career planning, 20

commitment, in MAPs process, 21

communication skills: augmented reality practice and, 74–76; and conflict resolution, 104–8, 106*t*–7*t*; and hidden curriculum, 82; proficiency levels, 50*t*; self-advocacy and, 120; small talk, 71, 87; tips for, 105*b*; understanding conversation, 66–67; what not to say, 84*t*–85*t*, 119; written, 38–43

companies hiring individuals with disabilities, 13, 34; resources on, 30

Comprehensive Transition and Postsecondary (CTP) program, 5–6

compromise, 107*t*

conflict on job, 93–111; ASD and, 93–95, 94*t*; emotional regulation and, 101–3; identification of, 95–98

conflict resolution: communication skills and, 104–8, 106*t*–7*t*; steps in, 96*t*–97*t*

consequences, role-playing, 89–90

contact information: on résumé, 44–45; in workplace, 87, 108

conversation, 66–67; small talk, 71, 87; sustaining, 67

coworkers: communication with, 84*t*–85*t*; conflict with, 98–99

CTP. *See* Comprehensive Transition and Postsecondary program

culture of workplace, 86; and dress, 70

curriculum, hidden. *See* hidden curriculum

customers: communication with, 85*t*; conflict with, 94, 100–101

disclosing disability, 15; in interview, 65–66; legal rights and, 114–15; pros and cons of, 66; role-play for, 66; self-determination and, 24; on social media, 37

diversity: and hidden curriculum, 80; respect for, 81–82

dream, in MAPs process, 20

dream jobs, 9; and goal setting, 25

dress, 70

dry runs, 67, 71–72. *See also* practice

EdPuzzle, 77*t*

education: and employment, 1; on résumé, 49

EEOC. *See* Equal Employment Opportunity Commission

email: and interview, 69; template for, 40

emotions: recognizing, 102*t*–3*t*; regulation of, 101–3

employee assistance program, definition of, 117

employer recommendations, 88, 121–22

employment: autism spectrum disorder and, 1–7; of autistic individuals, statistics on, 1–3; factors affecting success in, 5–7, 7*t*; value of, 1

Equal Employment Opportunity Commission (EEOC), 109, 114

equity, definition of, 116

essential job function, definition of, 116

etiquette, 105*b*; for interviews, 71–78

executive functioning impairment, and goal setting, 25

experience, relevant: activities for building, 56; on résumé, 47–48

eye contact, 71, 105*b*

Fast, Yvona, 15

Favorite Jobs Matrix, 30

feedback, 122

first impression, 68–71

Flipgrid, 77*t*

formal written communication, 38; characteristics of, 39*t*; identification of, 41–42

gender, and social cues, 84

goal setting, 24–26; activity on, 26–27

grammar, proficiency levels, 50*t*

greetings, 105*b*

Gut, D., 83

handbook, employee, 82, 107, 115, 117–18

handshakes, 71

harassment, 109–11; definition of, 116; sexual, 86, 95, 111

help requests, 107–8; for emotional regulation, 103–4, 103*t*

hidden curriculum, 79–91; coach on, 122; instruction strategies for, 83–90; nature of, 80–83

Higher Education Opportunity Act (HEOA), 5

high-functioning autism (HFA), 2

hostile work environment: definition of, 116; employer recommendations on, 121–22

human resources, 115

hygiene, 69; checklist for, 70

hyperfocus. *See* interests, intense

I Messages, 105–6

Immersive Simulations, 75, 76*f*–77*f*

inclusion: and career planning, 20; employer recommendations on, 121–22; transition and higher education programs and, 5–6

response, for emotional regulation, 102*t*, 103–4
résumé, 44–58; activities for building, 56; basic, 44–56; template for, 57; video, 56
retaliation, 119
retreat, for emotional regulation, 102*t*, 103–4
role-play: attitude, 87–88; disclosure, 66; interviews, 78; phone call, 69; picking up application, 43; and self-determination, 24; understanding questions, 72

self-advocacy, 120–21
self-assessments, 15
self-determination, 24
self-presentation, 43, 68–71, 86; checklist for, 70; on video résumés, 56
sensory issues, as workplace challenge, 4*t*
sexual harassment, 86, 95, 111
SIMmersion, 75, 76*f*–77*f*
Simpson, R. L., 109
skills: identification of, 52–54; proficiency levels, 50*t*–51*t*; on résumé, 49–51
small talk, 71, 87
SOCCSS Strategy, 88–90
social cues, in workplace, 84
social media, and networking, 37
social skills, 42–43; and networking, 35; as workplace challenge, 4*t*
Society for Human Resource Management, 115–16
soft skills, 42, 51; augmented reality practice and, 74–76; identification of, 54; on job, 79–91; and understanding questions, 72, 73*t*–74*t*
spelling, proficiency levels, 50*t*
Spheres of Influence, 35–36
STAR (Students Transitioning to Adult Roles) Process, 20–21,21*t*; chart tool, 22–23
story, in MAPs process, 20
strengths, and employment, 3–4, 5*b*; assessment of, 14–15; in interview, 68
success tips, 86–88; for workplace communication, 105*b*, 106*t*–7*t*
Sulaimani, M., 83

supervisors: communication with, 84*t*; conflict with, 99–100; recommendations for, 122

technology, for interview practice, 74–77, 76*f*–77*f*, 77*t*
terminology: in applications, 58, 59*t*; in job search, 62–63; in workplace, 116–17
Theory of Mind deficits, 72, 80, 83; and understanding questions, 72, 73*t*–74*t*
Thnk College, 6
time management, 42–43, 87
total compensation, definition of, 117
training: and employment success, 7; and listening skills, 72; on résumé, 49
transition planning, person-centered approach in, 20
transition services, 2–3; and employment success, 7

Underlying Characteristics Checklist (UCC-CL), 16
unemployment, ASD and, 80
University of Indiana, Autistic Job Recommendations, 30–31
U.S. Department of Labor, 113

video résumés, 56
voice, in STAR Process, 21
Voice Thread, 77*t*
volume, 84, 94, 105*b*

West Sussex County Council, 20
word processing skills, proficiency levels, 50*t*
workplace: communication tips for, 105*b*; conflict in, 93–111, 94*t*; hidden curriculum and, 79–91; policies in, 115–22
written communication, 38–43; formal versus informal, 39*t*, 41–42

Zielin, Lara, 35
Zoeller, Cindy, 34–37
Zoom, 77*t*

About the Authors

··

Patricia S. Arter is a professor of special education and the Department Chairperson of Counseling, Leadership and Educational Studies at Winthrop University in Rock Hill, South Carolina. She teaches graduate and undergraduate courses in special education. Dr. Arter's main areas of research are creating access for marginalized special needs populations through inclusion, behavior management, vocational training, social skills training, and Universal Design for Learning (UDL). Specifically, she has over a decade of experience working with individuals with autism spectrum disorder (ASD) in the areas of vocational training, social skills training, emotional regulation training, and use of virtual reality (VR) to improve interview training skills. Before moving to Winthrop University, she founded and directed (2007–2019) the SOAR program (Students On-Campus Achieving Results), an on-campus program for individuals with ASD to secure competitive employment. Dr. Arter has more than 20 peer-reviewed publications and national and international presentations in her research areas. In addition, she has been awarded over $300,000 in grants funding work with individuals with ASD. Prior to her career in higher education, Dr. Arter was an elementary and middle school teacher in inclusive classrooms for more than 15 years.

Tammy B. H. Brown is a professor in the School of Education at Marywood University. She teaches graduate and undergraduate courses in education and serves as director of the Students On-Campus Achieving Results (SOAR) program, a campus-based program to help individuals with ASD to secure competitive employment. She has published numerous practitioner-focused articles in state and national journals, including a recent article in Teaching Exceptional Children on the use of Virtual Reality (VR) to prepare individuals with ASD for job interviews. She has also presented at nearly 50 peer-reviewed conferences. She is a member of the Council for Exceptional Children (CEC), the International Literacy Association (ILA), the Society for Information Technology and Teacher Education (SITE), the International Dyslexia Association (IDA), and the Society of Children's Book Writers and Illustrators (SCBWI). She is also a member of the Keystone State Literacy Association (KSLA), where she has served on the journal's editorial board.

Jennifer Barna, PhD, NCC, ACS, is an associate professor and director of the school counseling program at Marywood University. She holds PK–12 school counseling

··

certification with an autism endorsement. Dr. Barna is a past president of both the Pennsylvania Counseling Association and the Pennsylvania Association of Counselor Educators and Supervisors. Her work with students on the autism spectrum includes several presentations on preparing students with ASD for the transition to college and supporting the social emotional development of students. She has also presented on how school counselors can support families who parent a child with ASD. Her most recent publications focus on helping students with ASD gain essential employability skills and making a successful transition to college. Dr. Barna is an advisory board member of the Students On-Campus Achieving Results (SOAR) program at Marywood University.

Made in the USA
Columbia, SC
24 August 2024

40970554R00083